GHOSTS OF
GONE WITH THE WIND

GENE ARCERI

Published in the USA by:
BearManor Media
PO Box 1129
Duncan, Oklahoma 73534-1129
www.bearmanormedia.com

ISBN 9781629337319

Cover Design by Chris Jones.
Book design by Brian Pearce | Red Jacket Press.

TABLE OF CONTENTS

For my niece, Barbra Ann Arcieri Carrier, a paranormal inquisiter.
And My Guardian Angel, T.F.C.S.

ACKNOWLEDGEMENTS

I stretched out a hand for help and found the 4-J's, who offered theirs in return: Joseph Marchi, James Kason, Jimmy Tayas and John Wiley ("The Scarlett Letter"). Virginia Cano extended hers, completing this hand-held partnership. If it were not for Sandra Grabman, BearManor Media's esteemed production manager, this book may have faded like a ghost itself. Sandy rescued it from that fate and held our hands throughout to completion, appreciating what is fleeting and what is enduring.

PROLOGUE

Give heed to what the echoing voices say,
Listen for footsteps from the past,
Note curiously the shadows cast
By presences that once were here
And now reappear — g.a.

"There is no present nor future. There is only the past happening over and over again," said Eugene O'Neill. If this be so, then pause, look behind you, and listen to the ghosts of voices in the wind. For once gone they will vanish like a dream.

I cannot say exactly when, or for that matter why, the odyssey for this book began, but the most auspicious of many possible beginnings was at the end of that day in the library. The most nebulous of things must enter life somewhere — in this case a darkened theater, where a thrilling spectacle unfolds on the screen, the vivid realism of the pageantry and drama enabling the viewer to transport himself to the very time and place he sees before him: the South during the Civil War, *Gone With the Wind*.

This fanciful flight of imagination and history was made possible because producer David O. Selznick had successfully integrated the diverse elements and efforts of hundreds of artists and technicians to create a masterpiece. That unique blend and Selznick's magic touch resulted in a living legend — unlocking the door to a world of enchantment and illusion for millions to find escape from a weary workaday world. Here they could lose the present and see yesterday, a world of not so long ago, forever gone, and join Scarlett in her determined vision of the future, "tomorrow...another day." Practically, everything about *GWTW* was extraordinary, and the encounters I shared were extraordinary in themselves. Something came about which was destined to bring it all into focus, and finally the scattered pieces of information all seemed to

9

fit together when I was introduced to the widow of the assistant director on *GWTW*.

This introduction to the widow would have never happened had it not been for former Broadway musical star and screen actress of the 1940s Irene Manning, best remembered for her role as Fay Templeton in *Yankee Doodle Dandy*. Irene had been under contract to Warner Bros.,

Gene in the Stacey home library.

where she worked under studio manager Eric Stacey, and became close friends with Eric and his wife Fran. Years later, Irene went to live in San Carlos, California to be near her second husband's business, but remained in close contact with the Staceys. After Eric's sudden death, Irene and Fran continued to exchange letters and telephone calls. It was on one of Irene's occasional visits in the spring of 1988 to see her old friend now

Left: *Vivien: 'Who was the lady I seed you with over there?' Eric: 'Shucks, that weren't no lady — that's Belle Watling!'* Right: *Fran Stacey.*

living in Solana Beach that I chanced to go along.

You could not help but like Fran Stacey at first sight. An attractive woman, Fran was as warm and gracious a host any stranger could ever hope to meet. Knowing beforehand, from Irene, of my interests in the movies, Fran made available to me all of her late husband's memorabilia, which had been stored in the garage for many years, so that I could browse through them while she and Irene caught up.

The late afternoon California sunlight filtered through the shutters of the library windows where the boxes sitting before me began to unfold the history of one man's life and his career in the motion picture industry before it was to end so tragically at a railroad crossing.

Among the treasures in front of me on the huge old library desk, one alone revealed more than any other the work of which this man was obviously most proud. A scrapbook more than a half-century old was stuffed with clippings, yellowing with age and crumbling like confetti around the edges, and was jammed with candid photographs and star biographical publicity sheets presenting a rare look into a period of film history. Private memories to be relived once it was all over. For when the screen credits unroll, wherever *GWTW* is showing, you will find the name "Eric G. Stacey, Assistant Director." A leather-bound, final-edition presentation

for Eric,
    who kept his sanity
    in spite of even
            NUT

with appreciation for a splendid job.

            Xmas, 1939.

Selznick's note to Eric, signed on Eric's personal script.

script was given to all of the GWTW principals as a Christmas gift by Selznick in 1939. To the Melanie of the picture, Selznick wrote in her script, "For Olivia, the Angel of Twelve Oaks, and Culver City, With great gratitude for her performance, and, more, for herself! Affectionately, David S. 1939 xmas." Beside his scrapbook was also a 1936 first edition of the Mitchell novel by The Macmillan Company. Turning back the

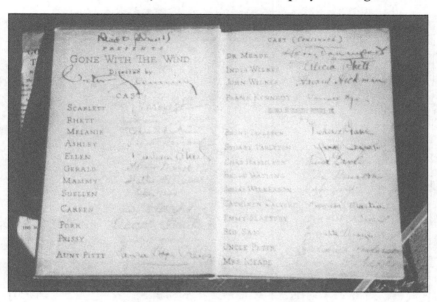

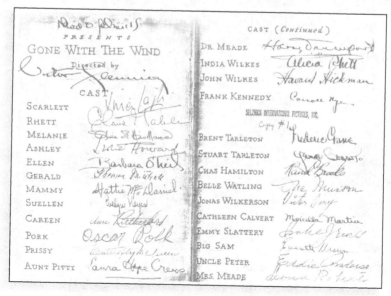

front cover of his scrapbook was like an insert appeared, reversing the years of a Movieola. Above the title *Gone with the Wind* on the top page was the signature of the film's producer, David O. Selznick. That page was followed by the margin signatures of Clark Gable, Vivien Leigh, and other members of the cast, reading like a Hollywood roll call of fallen soldiers. Alongside these riches was the leather-bound screenplay by

123 Ebano Court
Solana Beach, Cal.
Monday - March 14th

Dear Gene:

  Your thoughtful letter and enclosures were much appreciated. I called to thank you but you were not available ... so I called Irene and am looking forward to meeting you on the 26th of March here in Solana Beach (San Diego). It is kind of you to take the time to fly down and have a look at the material I have on "Gone With The Wind". There seems to be no end to the commercial ventures celebrating the 50th Anniversary of this memorable film...(note enclosure). You may take Eric's book of memorabilia home with you if you like. Irene will photograph whatever you need if you decide there is a story in this. I think I told you I have a first edition copy of GWTW with signatures of all cast members.... I wish I had more photographs.

  Anyway -- We'll have a good weekend and a change of pace.....looking forward to meeting you and seeing friend Irene again....

  Best to you.

  Fran

Letter to author from Fran Stacey.

Sidney Howard, inscribed by Selznick, "for Eric, who kept his sanity, in spite of even D.O.S. with appreciation for a splendid job, Xmas 1939."

Turner Entertainment Co. owns rights to *GWTW* and speaking at the 50th anniversary reunion in Atlanta, Ted Turner, the chief sponsor of the affair, said that, "if I were an alien from another planet, the film would be a textbook and primer in understanding human behavior. Not what happened in Tiananmen Square or the dropping of the Iron Curtain, but *Gone with the Wind.*" (GWTW)

IRENE MANNING

3165 LA MESA DRIVE
SAN CARLOS, CALIF. 94070
(415) 592-6045

5 June 92

Dearest Fran —

This is Gene Green's Book "VOICES GONE in the Wind" — a draft he wanted you to read + approve — and make any suggestions you deem fit.

He is doing the second half of the Book on the current effort in Film — so what you read is only the first half. Hope you like it. I think he has captured some rare dialogue from the people involved in the making of G.W.T.W. !

over →

CHAPTER ONE

WINDS OF FATE

In front of the soon-to-be conflagration stood a huge battery of flood-lights on tall platforms, and seven cameras with three men to each machine were positioned and trained upon the set. In the center of this assemblage the assistant director's microphone was positioned. The assistant director was a tall, sturdily-built, auburn-haired man of thirty-five with hazel eyes and a ruddy complexion. He presided over everything, wearing his inevitable hat, the Master of Ceremonies. His voice boomed above the throng of spectators, performers, grips, soundmen, electricians, cameramen, and every other technician known to the industry as he fine-tuned the preparations for this once-in-a-lifetime shot. He was a man at the peak of his profession.

Eric Glyn Stacey was born in Ramsgate, Kent, England on December 4, 1903. After attending private schools in England, he graduated high school in July 1921 and promptly went to work for Artistic Films, Ltd., at 93 Wardour St., London. He worked his way up to second assistant director on a series of features based on the works of W. W. Jacobs (e.g. *The Monkey's Paw* and other short stories). He made his first visit to the United States in 1923, and then returned to England on the SS Majestic. Anxious to return to America, and its budding motion-picture activities, he continued with Artistic Films, working on two reelers for the next two years before becoming assistant manager at the Regent Theatre in Brighton, with its 4,000 seats, three restaurants, dance hall and stage show.

In December 1925, Eric sailed back to New York on the S.S. Berengaria and, within months, the hard-working young man went from chief usher at the Rialto Theatre on Broadway to the New York production department of Famous Players-Lasky Corporation. Shortly after, the Lasky Corporation merged with Paramount Pictures Corporation and Eric moved out to the West Coast. He worked in Paramount's property department, until he met up with David O. Selznick, an anglophile, who hired him for his company. In 1935 Eric received an Oscar nomination from the Academy of Motion Picture Arts and Sciences for his work as assistant director on *Les Miserables* for 20th Century. The following year he was honored with another bid from the Academy for *The Garden of*

Allah, a Selznick production, and again in the same category in 1937, for Selznick on *A Star is Born.* He worked for Selznick from January 1936 until July 1940, when the company suspended operations. David O. Selznick expressed best what Eric had meant to him in a letter written at the time of their professional parting.

On December 10, 1938, Eric, a hair less than 6 feet at 190 pounds,

Eric Stacey's working chart for actors.

stood tensely awaiting the order to begin the greatest challenge of his career: the filming of the burning of the military supplies in Atlanta. The conflagration technically known as a "controlled fire" was to be overseen by a platoon of visiting firemen, who were ready to move if the occasion warranted. Just before the torches were to be applied, Selznick appeared. He had requested an observation platform be built for his guests. His widowed mother, Florence, was there, wrapped in a shawl, but his brother Myron was delayed at a dinner party. Selznick waited for more than an hour until he could wait no longer. Now Eric could proceed without delay. Selznick pushed one of the buttons on the keyboard-like console, which could regulate the flames in various parts of the holocaust. Seven Technicolor cameras were used to film the fires duplicating the actual scene of 75 years ago. Flames leaped 500 feet into the night sky. Ten pieces of equipment from the L.A. Fire Department, 25 policemen, 50 studio firemen and 200 studio helpers stood by. On Eric's order, fires carefully set by the special effects men burst into life and quickly spread, gobbling up the tinder box structures like they were cardboard. Three 5,000-gallon water tanks were used to douse the flames after the shooting wrapped.

SELZNICK INTERNATIONAL PICTURES, INC.

9336 WASHINGTON BOULEVARD   CULVER CITY, CALIFORNIA

January 9, 1940

DAVID O. SELZNICK
PRESIDENT

Mr. Eric Stacey
6445 Commodore Sloat Drive
Los Angeles, California

Dear Eric:

Please accept belatedly, but no less sincerely, my warmest thanks for your kind wire about "Gone with the Wind."

I do hope that the agonies that you suffered with us have some compensation for you in the final result, and that things will go as you want them to during the coming year. If there is anything at all that I can do to be helpful, please do not hesitate to call on me.

Sincerely,

dos:bb

Uninvited spectators got past the guards and stood mesmerized by the fire, waiting for the action to begin. The crowd of extras waited nearby, biting into their red apples left over from supper. At last the flames were just right, and Eric Stacey gave the cue. Never before had such a massive fire been staged in Hollywood. The glow of the leaping flames reflected from the low-hanging clouds that night. Citizens of Los Angeles and surrounding Hollywood, seeing the fire, got into their cars and drove toward the blaze. On another night explosions from the shells and ammunition sounded nervous Culver City residents to call the police department. "No," they were told, "an enemy fleet was not bombarding Long Beach." However, the fire in Selznick's eyes that night had as much to do with an unexpected visitor, so he believed, from London as the blazing sets. Olivia de Havilland, the last living woman of *GWTW* at age ninety-four, recalled that night. "I had not even been cast yet (as Melanie Hamilton). I lived in the Los Feliz district, and one night I was lying in bed and I saw the night sky light up in this terrible conflagration." She later learned that Eric Stacey's production crew had set fire to the old *King Kong* set to recreate the burning of Atlanta.

CHAPTER TWO

DAVID
(SELZNICK)
AND GOLIATH
(MITCHELL'S NOVEL)

On a quiet sunny morning in May 1936, a strange message arrived in Los Angeles for Selznick from his New York representative, Katherine (Kay) Brown. Having just finished reading an advance copy of a first novel written by an unknown author, Katherine went wild. In the call, she demanded that Selznick drop whatever he was doing at the time and spend the next 24 hours perusing 1,037 pages of an opus entitled *Gone With the Wind*. He must buy it at once, she insisted. He put the receiver down, deep in thought, and for the next few moments gazed out the window.

David O. Selznick, the son of film magnate Lewis J. Selznick (1810 — 1933), began his career by assisting his father in film production in New York, handling promotion and distribution. Lewis's early empire eventually collapsed, but the family name persisted for the next four decades as David created his own. In 1923, and after his father went bankrupt, David began to make documentaries. After a few failed ventures, he set out for Hollywood in 1926, where he was reluctantly hired by his father's former partner, Louis B. Mayer, for M-G-M's B-picture division.

He soon married Mayer's daughter Irene, and in 1933 moved into Irving Thalberg's old job as head of M-G-M production. He left M-G-M in 1935 to found his own company, Selznick International.

Selznick distinguished himself as producer of such quality classic films as *King Kong, Dinner at Eight, A Tale of Two Cities*, and many more. Kay Brown felt that the Margaret Mitchell novel was decidedly of that caliber and very much up to her boss' impeccable standards. Selznick had heard it all before — superlatives from agents, stars, directors, and the rest of the Hollywood Zoo, but not from the sweet, soft-spoken, mild-mannered Miss Brown. Once he was assured she was in her right mind, he listened to her about "that book." Eight weeks later on July 15, 1936, *[Author's note: Technically, the contract was signed July 30.]* he bought the motion picture rights to "that book" for the sum of fifty thousand dollars ($50,000). However, he thought he should have been put into a hospital — a first novel, an unknown author, all that money! Instead, he took a cruise to Honolulu while the author took to her bed.

Margaret Mitchell was born in Atlanta in 1900, into a prominent local family. Her father, Eugene Mitchell, was president of the Atlanta Historical Society and, under his influence, she developed an early interest in the Civil War. In 1926 a difficult ankle sprain caused her to leave her job as a journalist. Confined to her home she began work on her novel.

Home was a graceful three-story white house in Atlanta, the elegant Windsor house at 17 Crescent Avenue, which she lovingly referred to as "the dump!" From 1925-1932, Margaret Mitchell lived with her husband, John Marsh, in the basement apartment which looked out over Crescent Avenue. Most of the book had been completed by July 1928 but, until its publication in 1936, additional work was done in filling in missing chapters, rewriting others, and checking thousands of historical statements for accuracy. Her immortal characters were all brought to life in that apartment — the birthplace of *GWTW* at Windsor house, and literary history was made:

Rhett Butler, the dashing, cynical native of Charleston, openly consorts with the enemy and scoffs at patriotic ideals, marries Scarlett O'Hara, and finally walks out on her;

Scarlett, the sheltered Southern belle fighting for survival as her life of plantation ease crumbles around her;

Ashley Wilkes, the sensitive, impractical idealist and object of Scarlett's misplaced passion;

Melanie, the reticent, ladylike wife of Ashley, who dies young after having spent a hard life in devotion to her insecure husband and her belatedly appreciative sister-in-law, Scarlett.

As for its title, how did Mitchell come about it? A copy of Ernest Christopher Dowson (1867-1900) poems had been sent to Mitchell from Michael MacWhite of the Irish Legation in Washington, D.C. It has been suggested that Dowson may have found the phrase in one of James Clarence Mangan's poems while writing his own:

Solomon, where is the throne? It is gone with the wind.
Babylon! Where is the might? It is gone with the wind.
Like the swift shadows of Noon, like the dreams of the blind.
Vanish the glories and pomps of the earth in the wind.

She wrote from Atlanta to Mangan to thank him for his book. In her note, dated January 27, 1937, she mentioned that she had known nothing of Mangan's poems until after *GWTW*'s publication. At the time, she was even doubtful as to whether she wanted the novel published. "I wrote it for fun," she said, "If enough people want to spend three dollars [to buy the book] that will be fine." The result of the enormous stack of dusty copy paper, which had lain around her apartment covered with bath towels for so many years, was a Pulitzer Prize for Margaret Mitchell in May 1937. The certificate hung on the wall of her office, and she looked at it every day in wonderment.

Contrary to rumors persistent until her death and despite thousands of inquiries from frustrated fans, Mitchell had no intention of ever doing a continuation regarding the fate of Scarlett and Rhett. In the book, after Melanie dies, Scarlett appears diminished. The years of fighting to survive had been too much for her to carry on alone. Now she wanted someone to lean on, as Ashley and the others had leaned on her, and so she turned to Rhett. But he was leaving her, unwilling to risk the pain that inevitably resulted for anyone so foolish as to be in love with the impetuous Scarlett. This final blow was too much for her to take. She only wanted, then, to go home, back to Tara. As she set foot on the red clay soil of her beloved plantation, she was able to raise her head high again. The old fighting spirit came back into her Irish blood. She was determined that somehow, some way, she would recapture Rhett and rekindle his love. After all, didn't she have tomorrow? That is the way Mitchell ended her novel, and it was the way it would remain as long as she lived.

Following its tremendous success, no one bothered to ask Margaret Mitchell if she had written anything before *GWTW*. Two years after publication of her saga, while visiting friend Lois Cole Taylor one afternoon, she was encouraged to write another book. She said she might someday, when the fan mail had fallen off (she answered every letter and thanked every reviewer), the foreign editions were all published, and if her family and friends stayed well. Then a faraway look came into her blue eyes, and in her rich southern drawl she said, "You know, I always liked the book I wrote before *Gone With the Wind* better." (Margaret Mitchell had written, and destroyed, a novel of the First World War, describing the social impact on Atlanta of a nearby military base.) Lois took a firm grip on the arm of her chair and said, as calmly as she could, "How nice. And where is the manuscript now?"

Margaret smiled shyly, "Oh, I burned it up when I was finished. I just wrote it for fun. I never thought of having it published." And this was what she had often thought of doing with the manuscript of *GWTW*.

To date, *Gone with the Wind* has sold in numbers second only to *The Bible*, appearing on *The New York Times* Best Seller lists in 1936 and again in 1992, both in hardcover and paperback editions. Herb Bridges, a letter carrier from Newman, in the rural countryside of Georgia about forty miles from Jonesboro, was unique in his interest in the novel and the movie. Bridges owned hundreds of copies of the novel in about forty languages, including rare pirated editions published in Mexico, Turkey and Greece. His major frustration had been his failure to find a Russian edition, which he was certain existed because Mrs. Nikita Khrushchev, on her visit to the U.S. in the 1970s, declared that she had read the novel three times. *[Author's note: Herb later acquired many Russian editions.]* One wonders whether Mr. Bridges had the thirty-volume Braille version.

Mitchell wrote from Atlanta to Dr. Wallace McClure, a U.S. Government literary copywriter official at the State Department in Washington D.C., thanking him for his offer of a pirated edition of *GWTW* "...it will round out my collection of foreign editions and it is all I will ever get out of China, I suppose."

Her brother, Stephens Mitchell, who was also her attorney, was ever on the alert to protect his sister's book from pirated editions in China, Holland, and elsewhere. During World War II the novel was banned by the Nazis, but in Poland and other occupied countries it was used by resistance fighters to build morale. In 1941 Mitchell won a suit in the Dutch courts against an unauthorized edition, thus establishing a significant legal precedent.

In November 1991, Simon & Schuster released more than 100,000 copies of its audio version, a record first. The Heritage Club published a special beautifully- illustrated two-volume edition of the book. The U.S. Postal Service issued a block of four commemorative stamps spot-lighting *GWTW*, to honor classical films from Hollywood. With these releases, millions of Americans found escape and inspiration from the lingering tail end of the Great Depression by experiencing how a devastated plantation family survived disaster; the family held together by its willful and indemonstrable heroine. As the depression dragged on, America was obsessed with escapism, and Hollywood's panacea was its dream factory. *GWTW* hit a chord of "triumph over the odds," and won a place in movie history which it has never lost. *[Author's note: On the October 31, 2008 episode of Jeopardy, a TV quiz show seen by millions, asked the final jeopardy question of its three young contestants on GWTW, and all three answered correctly.]*

Today *GWTW* belongs to the world, having been translated into about forty languages and sold in more than fifty countries. Former Communist regimes, which once banned *GWTW* because of the glorification of individuality and enterprise, now eagerly await the debut of the 1939 movie in their own countries. Tourists from Japan to Norway seek out "Taraland" in the never-ending search for the antebellum South of mansions and magnolias, when cotton was king, and Scarlett was fighting to endure and rebuild Tara, trying to hold on to both the traditions of the Old South that were swept away by the Civil War, and on to Rhett who would be swept away by her intransigence. "There's a nostalgic feeling among the Japanese people for the Old South" said Yuriko Meguro, a Japanese sociologist who specializes in American Culture. "Japanese identify with Georgia because of their attachment to *GWTW*." Coca-Cola executives in the US claim that Sankuru Inc., an alcoholic beverage producer, began selling California wine with a scene from *GWTW* on its label.

In July 1939, Margaret Mitchell wrote another letter to Dr. Wallace McClure about an unauthorized Japanese edition of *GWTW*. She had received a paperback, three-volume, board-bound Japanese translation of her novel, with a letter from the translator. Apart from the illegalities, which he certainly did not mention, he wrote of the popularity of the book, which so far had outsold Pearl S. Buck's *The Good Earth*. When Mitchell, through her lawyers, demanded royalties, she received a silk kimono and a Japanese doll in return with a request. "They wanted a picture of me standing by the Japanese doll wearing the kimono so that they could use it for publicity purposes. A nation with so much gall should go far. Needless to say, they will not get the picture." A year later she wrote to McClure about rumors of a pirated movie of *GWTW* being produced in Japan. Although she sympathized with Selznick in aborting such an attempt, nevertheless she was amused by the prospect, "Still, I would like to see a Japanese movie of my novel; the Japanese Confederates would doubtless be marching forth to defend Atlanta in Samurai armor, and Scarlett would be dashing about in a rickshaw instead of a buggy." Be that as it may, uncompromising Selznick would conform to the demands of Western Culture. David would face his Goliath…his way!

CHAPTER THREE
FACES

Selznick knew he had come face to face with his visualization of the ideal of his Scarlett O'Hara. The visitor during the filming of the Atlanta fire, the former Vivian Mary Hartley (Vivien Leigh) *[Author's note: She was born "Vivian," with an "a," but began using as her stage name "Vivien," with an "e"]*, was exquisite to look at. But this willowy-waisted stray from England was capable of unleashing a flow of profanity in total opposition to her demure appearance which was all the more shocking to strangers. She was an artist to her fingertips. From the time this convent-schooled daughter of a wealthy stockbroker was seven years old, the stage had been her first love. She wanted to be an actress. But being an actress would be overpowered once she met Laurence Olivier. From the beginning of her career, she courted scandal and continued to do so by following Olivier, with whom she had fallen madly in love while co-starring with him in the 1937 film *Fire Over England*, to Hollywood. Each having left behind a spouse and a child.

Olivier recalled: "Apart from her looks, which were magical, she possessed beautiful poise; her neck looked almost too fragile...she also had something else: an attraction of the perturbing nature I had ever encountered." The moment that two people destined for each other first become aware of this bewitchment, a mysticism is in the air.

Speaking of her first visit to America, Vivien said, "I had come to Hollywood for a week to visit friends (Laurence Olivier — singular), and during that week two things happened. I'd witnessed the biggest fire I had ever seen, the burning of Atlanta, at Mr. Myron Selznick's invitation (also Olivier's agent). Then the same evening his brother David, the producer of the picture, asked if I would like to test for the role of Scarlett." It wasn't quite that innocent. Vivien would have been more surprised if he had not asked her to test — according to Olivier and his agent's plan. In fact, in the late autumn of 1938, in London, Vivien grieved over her separation from the man she adored. She bade him a sad farewell aboard the Normandy on Saturday November the 5th, when he left New York for passage to Hollywood to film *Wuthering Heights*, the picture in which he had fought, and failed, to have her as his co-star.

After a barrage of letters from him telling of his troubles in Hollywood during the making of the film, she could bear it no longer. Olivier, meanwhile, threatened to withdraw from the Bronte classic, unless his beloved Vivien replace Merle Oberon, doubtless endearing himself to Oberon no end. Determined to be with him, with less than a three-week break between engagements, she sailed from Southampton on the Queen Mary on November 29th, having booked an expensive flight from New York to Hollywood, since travel time would leave only five days with Larry.

In his biography of Charles Laughton (Grove Press 1987), author Simon Callow wrote about Vivien Leigh "…she contains within her a spirit of anarchy, a real danger and unpredictability, that is *Lu Lu* like, a demon, a siren, a pussycat with the sharpest claws and a tongue that spits like a lynx." Laughton didn't care much for her either, and particularly didn't like to hear profanity used by someone who belonged to the same sex as his mother.

Selznick had had an opportunity to view her work in *Fire Over England*, 1936, with Olivier, again in 1937 in *A Yank At Oxford* and her latest *St. Martin's Lane*, 1938, her most insolent performance. Having had that chance to pass on her three times on celluloid. When he met the reject head-on, in the flesh, he discovered she really was Scarlett. It was not just a toss of the dice. Also, the casting of Scarlett was down to the wire. He had to begin shooting — with or without Scarlett — as M-G-M had loaned him Gable for only twenty weeks, after which he had to report back to his home studio. Selznick could fiddle around no longer — and so Atlanta burned.

The countdown began. "It was now December 21st and the day I went out to the studio for the test," Vivien said, "Scarletts were walking around all over the place."

"Hurry out of that costume," the wardrobe woman ordered, "There are other Scarletts waiting to use it!"

George Cukor, the director, had a busy day that Wednesday, rehearsing final contenders Joan Bennett and Paulette Goddard. Oh, yes, and the new girl. *GWTW* press agent Russell Birdwell warned Selznick the girl who got the role must be prepared to have her life laid bare in cold, black type. Goddard certainly could not stand up to the scrutiny of the media. Paulette (who was Jewish) lived the high life and died in 1990 the merry widow of German novelist, Erich Maria Remarque, best known for his powerful look at another war, *All Quiet On The Western Front*. After his death, Paulette moved to Switzerland. She died spectacularly rich, leaving twenty million dollars to New York University to benefit the arts. A final true-to-form gesture from the classiest good-time girl in the world.

On the brink of uncertainty, Vivien was all too aware of Paulette's influence with the Selznick brothers, and any other man that she needed. A half-hour before it was her turn on the test soundstage, trying to be casual about it all, she whispered to herself as she looked into the mirror,

"You haven't a chance in a million, so you might as well enjoy it!" An incident only talked about much later. After the test scene, with Mammy helping Scarlett dress for the barbecue, tugging the corset strings "tight enough to achieve the smallest waist in the county," she recalled "they gave me two additional scenes to learn, one of them the encounter between Scarlett and Ashley in the library of the Twelve Oaks Plantation and the scene in the woodshed at Tara where, for the last time, she begs Ashley to run away with her.

"So as my first experience in front of American cameras," she laughed, "I stormed about, punched pillows, threw vases and at the end the director said, 'Okay, you'd better go get some lunch now...NEXT!'" The test would prove conclusively that Vivien was the superior embodiment of Scarlett. Afterwards, she thanked Leslie Howard for his help and support. He thought her amazingly effective — arrogant even — no drippy magnolia coyness about Miss Leigh. She might be manipulative but she was never coy. One day during a take as Scarlett, she was to say, "Oh, fiddle-dee-dee." Instead she said, "Oh, fiddle-dee-fuck," then looked at her director in all innocence. It wasn't a slip; she just didn't want Cukor to print that particular take. Her naughtiness just endeared her to Cukor, who was gay, all the more.

This fragile beauty was not above using the raunchiest language when it suited her, especially when she lost her temper (she was a Scorpio). It always came as a great shock to those hearing it for the first time, coming from someone otherwise so prim and proper. Rex Harrison was quoted as saying, "She was very like a cat. She would purr and she would scratch and she looked divinely pretty doing it."

Beyond her obsession about Scarlett, her abiding passion was Olivier. He was truly the only thing that mattered. "Tomorrow" for Vivien came on that Christmas day, December 25, 1938, at the Sunday luncheon held at George Cukor's home in honor of the beautiful, unconventional, romantic unmarried British couple. The studio could gloss over the fact that Vivien had left her husband and child and was living with Olivier — after all, they were foreigners. At this time Cukor was engaged in the preliminary shooting arrangements for *GWTW*. From the beginning Selznick had chosen his crony Cukor, 39, who resembled him, to direct the picture.

A native New Yorker, Cukor had entered the theatre as an actor, in his teens. By 1926 he was directing such stars as Ethel Barrymore, Jeanne Eagles and the unforgettable Laurette Taylor on Broadway. In 1929 he joined the mass exodus (in part due to the Great Depression) of Broadway talent to a Hollywood, undergoing the big switch to sound movies. Cukor's professional association with Selznick, which began in New York years earlier, resulted in such memorable films as *Dinner at Eight, Little Women* and others. He had just completed *Camille* with Garbo. At his beautiful home on Cordele Street on the fringe of Beverly Hills, during the Christmas luncheon with a few close friends — including Garbo — he suddenly leaned forward and said, "Well, Vivien, I guess we are stuck with you." Just like that, she remembered, "as matter of fact, as if he had said, 'Well, Vivien, have some more turkey.'" For a moment she didn't take it seriously, certain she had heard it wrong — a Christmas joke? American style! When it finally sank in, she laughed and cried at the same time, proving that the power of the dream is largely generated by the fact that every now and then it comes true. She was divinely happy, and Olivier was happy for her, yet fearful of the consequences her sudden fame might have on his power over her. Torn between pride and apprehension, at certain stages he even tried to block her getting the part. Still, it was not too late — the contract had yet to be signed.

It came down to either signing or losing Scarlett altogether. After long days and nights of contract negotiations and heated discussions with Olivier, Vivien finally signed on Friday, January 13 (an unlucky number as we shall see), 1939. *[Author's note: Leigh, Howard and de Havilland signed their contracts on Friday, January 13.]* She wore a simple dress, her lucky lion and unicorn brooch. It was a fateful day for the superstitious English girl whose physical and emotional health would never be the same again and an unlucky day for the dozen of hopeful Scarletts who wept with disappointment — except for one dry -eyed youngster from Brooklyn (definitely superstitious) who felt that the outcome was planned all along. Edith Marrener tested many times with all the aspiring Ashleys. Undefeated she fought her way to an Academy Award as the re-named Susan Hayward. Asked about the experience by reporter Steve Warren, at the premier of her final motion picture *The Revengers* in Atlanta in 1972, Hayward said, as if excusing herself from not getting the part, "It would have been the shortest career on record. I was 16½ (19 actually) years old and I didn't know where the camera was. I was one amongst many who were brought here (Hollywood) — sort of a publicity thing. I think they knew all along who was gonna play Scarlett." (In retrospect this seems highly unlikely).

Still, Edith Marrener/Susan Hayward was not forgotten. Margaret Mitchell wrote to M-G-M's Kay Brown in New York on December 10, 1937, a year before Vivien Leigh was officially given the part of Scarlett.

"I haven't mentioned the young lady you told me about over the phone and will not of course (confidentiality was required). I had immediately forgotten her name." [She was referring to Edith Marrener, whom Irene Selznick had discovered at a fashion show. The young redhead began as a New York model.] "Of course," Mitchell continued, "I'd love to know what happened to her and I think it would be grand if you did telephone me about it."

Director Henry Hathaway had this to say to me about Hayward's rejection for the part, "The biggest disappointment in her life that, maybe, set her off was she thought she was going to be Scarlett. She was shaken by it. They wanted some new person — what the hell — Vivien Leigh was unknown. (But experienced on stage and film in England). She (Hayward) would have been equally as good as Vivien Leigh playing the part. Selznick didn't care at that time who it was, just so she was beautiful, brilliant and full of belligerence — and she (Hayward) was! She was Scarlett if there ever was one. She was an instinctively good actress — and she could have handled it." (Hathaway later directed Hayward in several films at 20th Century Fox.) Hathaway overlooked one decisive factor that day he spoke to me about it — Hayward didn't have Selznick's powerful brother as her agent.

At last, two weeks before filming began, the female lead had been decided upon. Ending an eighteen-month search for the would-be-Scarlett, "Cinderellas" were auditioned until the glass slipper finally fit. Meanwhile, en route to New York by rail, Selznick encountered a Mrs. Freeman, an ardent southerner who was incensed at his betrayal of the south. Mrs. Freeman cornered the producer in his compartment and verbally pounded away at him to change his mind and hire a Southern girl instead of this English upstart. When she paused long enough to draw breath, Selznick seized the opening and jumped in, "Mrs. Freeman," he said, "in these two years I've had my doubts. I've considered Southern girls — but I've been listening to you for an hour, and I haven't understood a god dammed word you've said."

About Clark Gable! This brief — (excerpt) will introduce another key person I was destined to meet linked with *GWTW*. Compelled to write a book about Susan Hayward after her passing, in 1981, I was trying to interest a British publisher in my manuscript, and found myself aboard a British Airways flight to London. Once airborne, I looked to change my seat on the aircraft and spotted some vacant seats toward the rear of the plane. I enquired of a late — middle-aged lady seated in an aisle seat whether or not the adjoining seats in her row were occupied. She looked up from her book and revealed herself to be a pretty lady with white hair, light blue eyes, tastefully dressed in a medium gray suit. In friendly tones she said they were not and would be pleased to have my company. Before the plane landed at Heathrow we had become sufficiently acquainted that we decided to stay in touch. During the flight I told her of my search for a British publisher. To my surprise she let it be known that her boss had made a movie with the Hayward actress. So I met the most lasting relationship in Clark Gable's life from 1939-1960. She became his secretary, major domo and business manager at the peak of his career. In 1934 he won an Oscar for *It Happened One Night* while on loan-out from M-G-M, his home studio. He would reign, by reputation, as the hard living King of the movies for the next 30 years, carving quite a reputation as a party animal, even dating Nancy Davis before she met Ronald Reagan. He took all the acclaim in his stride, "I'm just a lucky slob from Ohio. You step into Hollywood; you wind yourself into thousands of chains of accidents. If all the thousands come out exactly right then you'll be a star."

His former loyal associate and friend, Jean Garceau, now a widow, was living in Walnut Creek, at a retirement center, just twenty miles from San Francisco She had only just moved to Northern California after selling her home in Sherman Oaks. Jean not only became a good friend but tried to help me place the Susan Hayward book. She was in London to do a BBC special for Barry Brown; the Production Chief of *The Hollywood Greats* series, seen on PBS, Jean was part of the Clark Gable segment.

Back home in California she invited me to visit her at her lovely cottage in Rossmore, Marin County. She prepared a brunch similar to one she had so often done for the Gables. Scrambled eggs, grits, sausage, biscuits, jam and coffee. We sat in the dining room on furniture given to her by them, surrounded by countless gifts of other fine country furniture and china from Clark and Carole. After lunch Jean gave me a special tour of her home. The photographs that lined the hallway were most unusual. "Clark," she said, pointing to one, "was the most glamorous man in the world." She had the narrative of Lombard and Gable's lives mounted in albums piled up in her closet. They had gathered no dust as she often glanced through them. In the bedroom, above the twin beds, were two wooden plaques that the Gables had given her and her husband Russ. She opened her jewelry case to show some of the gifts given to her over the years; a gold necklace given to Carole by Marlene Dietrich, a handcrafted silver and amethyst necklace, bracelet and ring chosen by Clark. Later as we sat in the sunroom overlooking rolling green lawns, Jean with Chatty, her little white Schnauzer on her lap, told me how she came to Rossmore.

She had lost her husband Russ after fifty years of marriage. Jean and her husband had built their dream home in Sherman Oaks. The hilltop site where they planned to build would be closer to both their jobs. Influenced by the Early American style of the Gable's home, they designed a grey shingle Cape Cod. Carole and Clark saw the plans, liked them so much they decided to build a similar house for Clark's father. They visited the Garceaus' every Sunday to check on the progress, Carole serving as decorating consultant. The Gables gave them the white marble for their bathroom and counter tops, and all of their dining room furniture. When Gable's father moved into his house Carole told Jean, "Pa" (her pet name for Clark) had such a bad time of it with father Gable when he was a boy, it's a joy for him to be on good terms with his Dad."

With her house on the market, one day Jean showed it to "a little woman, rather quiet, very discreet," who fell in love with it. Jean felt immediately that this was the woman she wanted to have her home. Bette Midler lived there for years.

Jean Garceau began her business career with Myron Selznick, David's older brother. Myron was Hollywood's first talent agent to exert great leverage on studio affairs through his control over a roster of top people in demand. Jean prepared income taxes, paid bills, found servants for them; and among her personal accounts was Carole Lombard. Lombard, a pal to all on the set, was dearly loved by her buddies. A tomboyish prankster with a longshoreman's mouth, she had a natural gift for laughter. Beautiful, blonde, Carole Lombard hit her stride as a star in the mid 1930s when, by sheer vitality and keen intelligence, she turned screwball comedy into an art. Carole phoned the Myron Selznick Agency and asked Jean to bring some papers to her home that she shared with her mother, Bessie, and her two brothers in Bel Air. When Jean arrived she heard music and laughter coming from the living room. When she was shown in she saw Carole teaching a dance routine to a familiar handsome man, Clark Gable. After being introduced, she told him, "I've always liked someone who has a good firm handshake," and he did! Carole had left the room and he was standing where she had left him. Jean wondered what she should say to him. The news in the trade papers was that Selznick had cast him for Rhett Butler. He had, too, in response to the overwhelming barrage of letters from women across the country, demanding that he play that part and no one else, so she led in with that as a reference.

"Well," she said, "you must be pretty excited about starring in *GWTW.*"

"No, I'm not! I'm scared to death. I've read the book several times, trying to feel my way into the character. I hope I can do justice to him."

"Nobody else could do it," Jean replied, "Look at all the fans who have written because they want to see you in that part."

"That's just the trouble. I've got millions of women to please."

At first, Gable was reluctant to play Rhett Butler. He knew that the public, after reading the bestselling novel, had a preconceived idea of the kind of Rhett Butler they expected to see on the screen. "Suppose I come up empty? Suppose I don't produce?" Upon first reading the book, he had reacted enthusiastically with, "What a part for Ronald Colman." Author Mitchell liked the idea of Gary Cooper. Fortunately, he had little choice as to whether or not he would play Rhett. His M-G-M contract did not allow him to select his own parts. The studio was in total control of his career. Gable's contract for *GWTW* was signed on August 24, 1938, albeit conditionally — no southern accent. He was also concerned about the fit of the costumes, and was used to working with one particular tailor whom Selznick had to hire to correct a contractual oversight. Gable began rigorous preparations. "I started out with the idea of knowing Rhett as well as I knew myself. I lived with him day after day, reading and rereading *GWTW*, underlining each sentence that revealed a facet of his many sided character." Jean confirmed this, "He put in months of unrelenting preparation from August 1938 to actual filming in January 1939."

Jean later realized that Carole had arranged the meeting in her living room to get Clark's opinion about Jean's replacing her present live-in secretary and friend, Madalynne Fields, who was leaving to get married. At first she hesitated. "My husband and home came first," Jean repeated.

Lombard persisted and Jean took the chance and resigned from Myron Selznick, starting her new job in an office in Carole's home. In the twenty-one years that followed she acquired a very personal and privileged look at Lombard and Gable.

When the romance of Clark and Carole began in 1936 they were both major stars, the ultimate glamour symbols of America. He was thirty-five years old, she was twenty-seven. Both had unsuccessful marriages. They were highly developed personalities with very different approaches to life: Carole was generous, easy going and sensitive. She also had a lot of creative friends and pals from the crews of many of her movies. On the other hand, Gable was insecure, stubborn and penurious, yet between them existed a spirit of youthful fun and happiness that prevailed from their first moment together. Photographer John Engstead, one of Carole's closest gay friends from the Hollywood 1920's, told me, in the Redwood Room of the Clift Hotel, in San Francisco, that except for her childhood the longest completely happy time in her life was when she and Gable fell

in love. He admitted Carole knew every swear word uttered and made up
a few of her own to use around the studio; mostly to keep amorous executives at bay. But she never swore in front of her mother, Jean Garceau or
Clark because they were offended by such talk. Carole filled Gable's life
with fun and laughter. When he was silent or moody, she would clown
around until he smiled again. And they were both practical jokers.

*Carole Lombard and Clark Gable have eyes only for each other, missing the
horse race.*

Love was in the air, it seems, for it was during the making of *GWTW*
that assistant director Eric Stacy began dating Frances Eugenie Stinnette
from Evington, Virginia. Fran was Will Hays' secretary, the watchdog of
morality on film, who was appointed by the major Hollywood studios
in 1922 to head their new organization, The Motion Picture Producers
and Distributors of America, Inc., designed to improve the image of
the industry, following increasing highly publicized scandals. It was, in
effect, the creation of an office of film censorship. In 1930 the MPPDA,
then known as the Hays Office, created a moral code, perilously missing
today, that fundamentally molded the content and image of Hollywood
films until 1966.

On January 13, 1939, Leslie Howard signed to play Ashley Wilkes.
He had never liked the part of Ashley (who was modeled after Margaret
Mitchell's first love, Clifford Henry — a poetry spouting romantic who
was killed during World War 1, reflected in Scarlett's true love, the sensitive and intelligent Ashley Wilkes). Howard never bothered to read the
book, and only agreed to do it after Selznick promised to allow him to

Leslie Howard as Ashley Wilkes.

direct some films at the Selznick Studios. Living up to his promise Selznick gave him the role of the violin virtuoso in *Intermezzo*, in addition to director and associate-producer assignments. When he saw his test as Ashley Wilkes, heavily made-up and partially be-wigged, wearing a Confederate Uniform, he remarked, "I look like a fairy doorman at the Beverly Hills Hotel."

Born Leslie Howard Steiner in London, England, in 1893, he had made his reputation as a stage actor in 1920 and remained behind the footlights, mostly in New York, for more than a full decade until, at age thirty-seven, he starred in his first movie, *Outward Bound*. Slender, blue-eyed, with blond curly hair above a very high forehead, to Americans he was the quintessential upper-class Britisher. To his compatriots he was something of an imposter, having been born in humble circumstances to Hungarian immigrant parents.

The competition for the black roles, especially that of Mammy, was intense. Bets were all on Louise Beavers, who had captured everyone's heart as the flapjack-making partner of Claudette Colbert in the 1934 weeper, *Imitation of Life*. As the joyous, big black Mammish Aunt Jemima, she appeared to be a natural for the part of Mammy in *GWTW*. Louise and Hattie often competed for the same parts, but remained life-long friends. Director George Cukor was besieged by colleagues on Louise's behalf. It's been said, however, that in her first interview for the part at Selznick International, Miss Beavers walked in all done up, wearing her most elegant furs, rather out of character for the ruling housekeeper of Tara. Nevertheless, she did test for the part.

From the White House came a suggestion which could not be ignored. Eleanor Roosevelt wrote to Selznick offering White House cook Elizabeth McDuffie for the role. And so Miss McDuffie tested as well. Letters came from everywhere about other "Mammys" while Hattie patiently read *GWTW*, feeling instinctively that she was the right one. Bing Crosby, who felt the same about her, wrote to Selznick personally to say so.

In December 1938 *[Author's note: This was after the fire sequence was shot on December 10]*, Hattie tested for Mammy with Vivien Leigh, in the scene from the beginning of the motion picture where Mammy is lacing a corset onto Scarlett and fussing because Scarlett had been 'gobbling like a hawk,' running the risk of gaining unwanted weight. She also counsels her against making a fool of herself over Ashley Wilkes, the object of Scarlett's infatuation. Making full use of her voice, some rolling southern shuffle and a loud thick Georgian accent, Hattie said, "I did my best and God did the rest." Dialect expert, Susan Myrick, hired for the picture, disagreed. In a letter to Margaret Mitchell, dated January 15, 1939, she wrote: "Hattie Mc Daniel is not the right Mammy — she lacks dignity, nobility and she hasn't the right face for it." (In time she retracted her words, and she and Hattie became friends.)

Vivien knew how crucial the test was for Hattie, and how important a part McDaniel played in making her look her best. She also felt Hattie

Hattie 'Mammy' McDaniel.

was lucky for her and many believed she helped Hattie land her role. Vivien always had the greatest warmth and affection for her, and Hattie, a natural entertainer would often brighten her day when she was low and missing Olivier; Hattie would soon have her smiling again. On January 27, 1939, Selznick signed Hattie for the part of Mammy. Hattie could often be found under the big oak tree on the Tara set with the actors who were playing Pork, Jeems and Prissy, (the house servants in the film) gathered around her while at her feet sat a boy of ten looking all of the 'pickanniny' (little black children of slaves) he was in the picture. They would laugh and talk but Hattie had a script on her lap going over her lines, mumbling them out loud pursing her lips and rolling her eyes around. One day at noon Vivien walked over to her and asked in her thickest Miss Scarlett drawl, "Mammy may ah go at lunch?" and Mammy in her most Mammish way answered, "Where yo goin'?" They both laughed as Vivien pranced away.

Vivien gave mischievous impersonations of the cast and production executives, using very bogus accents, with as many four-letter words as she could contrive — shocking Mammy McDaniel. Vivien delighted in telling friends, "During the first days of shooting, any visitor to the set would have suspected that Olivia (de Havilland) and I were muzzy-minded. We went around muttering to each other phrases like 'fo-o-ur door Fooord — I can't afford a four door Ford. I can't dance in fancy pants.' All to get the proper intonation in our southern accent. Under the guidance of jolly Sue Myrick, of Macon, Georgia, we dripped honey on our words but carefully. For Sue was liable to say in the middle of a shot, 'That's too Southern dear!' And back we'd scurry to practicing 'four door Fords.'"

Vivien, a tiny figure, whose weight hovered around a 100 pounds, and only a couple of inches above five feet, drove herself relentlessly to meet the strenuous demands made on her. Eric noted in his daily log, "in that entire time she worked on that picture for 22 weeks, with only 4 days off making her role, up to 1939, the longest most intensive in film history. Her more than 40 costume changes were also the largest wardrobe any player had ever had in one production. Her salary for playing Scarlett, perhaps the most coveted role in Hollywood history, was somewhere in the region of $30,000. In addition to being on the set 12-15 hours a day, 6 days a week, she had the pressure of being in a different country, speaking in a different accent from her own and spending hours in intense heat and dust. 20 tons of bricks had been pulverized to simulate the red dust of Georgia. She spent long days breathing in this stifling air and never missed a day shooting."

"After so many months, all of us were anxious to complete the picture to see what we had," she said. "I drank quarts of milk with honey in it to keep up weight, snatched sleep between shots, ploughed through gore and battle smoke and 'the red dust of Georgia.' I swing between happiness and misery and I cry easily. I'm a mixture of my mother's determination and father's optimism. I'm part prude and part non-conformist. I say

Scarlett and Rhett — a moment of truce.

what I think. I'm a mixture of French, Irish and Yorkshire and perhaps that's what it all is."

She could be difficult under the strain, but she was always the professional. True, she was not popular with everyone in the cast and crew. She identified so closely with the part of Scarlett that when I asked Evelyn Keyes (who played her sister) during an interview what Vivien Leigh was really like off camera, she could only say, "She WAS Scarlett!" On the set Vivien would fret over the interminable delays. "What are they fucking around for?" There were often long periods of inactivity during lighting and set changes, during which de Havilland would distract her in a corner of the set, playing a popular game of the time called Battleship, a derivative of checkers. Of course Vivien loved it when she won, which she often did. What never ceased to amaze Olivia de Havilland was her capacity to rise from the game, then after being checked by the make-up man — go directly to the set and immediately transform herself into character to shoot the scene. Unlike Olivia, who told me (during a 1970s interview for PBS in San Francisco) she would have to stop beforehand, like many performers in major roles, return to her dressing room for a good fifteen minutes to get back into character.

One day Vivien found Hattie on the set moving her lips, jiggling her feet and laughing to herself. "What on earth are ya up to, Mammy?" she asked. Hattie replied that she was writing an act for the time that she might go on a personal appearance tour. To demonstrate, Mammy went into a tap dance, humming in her lush contralto voice. She kicked, did steps, rolled her eyes in rhythm with her dance routine. Vivien was her best audience.

Hattie McDaniel, born in Wichita, Kansas June 10, 1895 was the 13th child of a Baptist minister. She was 'inspired' to go into show business, she said, by winning a gold medal in dramatic art presented by Denver's White Women's Christian Temperance Union. She sang with bands and made it to vaudeville. When no theatrical or film bookings were to be had, she worked as a ladies room attendant. A total lack of movie work in the 1920s and early 1930s made it necessary for her to take in washing, but a long memory of some of her good work for Selznick in some of his earlier movies led to her getting the part in *GWTW*. One of Hattie's favorite scenes from the movie was of the defeated homeward-bound Confederate soldiers stopping by Tara for rest and food: real Southern corn pone, turnip greens, dry salt pork and sweet potatoes. When the studio commissary sent out box lunches of chicken sandwiches that day, the delivery man found the entire cast dining on soul food. Hattie, who joined Vivien and Gable in the feast, proclaimed "The old Southern standby had won out over a Hollywood diet and many of the box lunches were returned to the cafeteria unopened."

Another scene Hattie enjoyed had Mammy and Rhett having a drink, celebrating Bonnie Butler's birth, drinking colored water. After many retakes Hattie told Gable, "I sure am tired of drinking colored tea." Gable

Aunt Pitty helping to celebrate Ashley's birthday.

got a look in his eye, then spoke to his valet, who left and returned shortly. Ready for another take, the director yelled, "Lights, Camera, Action!" and Hattie took a large swig of her drink. Instead of tea she downed a big gulp of scotch, breaking up the scene and all present. "The very idea of him [Gable] playing that kind of a trick on poor ole Mammy." Eventually McDaniel did go on tour for *GWTW*, and included many such stories, with songs and dances in the skit "Mammy's Meditations," which she did for the audiences.

A full copy of "Mammy's Meditations" is with the Selznick Papers at the University of Texas, in Austin.

Aunt Pitty was played by Laura Hope Crews, one of the many veteran actors in the picture. Harry Davenport, who played kindly Dr. Meade, began his stage at age five one year after the Civil War. Miss Crews was born in San Francisco on December 12, 1879 (fourteen years after the

Civil War ended) making her stage debut at age four. During production she had a record made of Mrs. Wilbur Kurt's voice so she could study it for the Southern accent and tone. During the filming Miss Crews lost her longtime companion (who had been her personal maid). Following two sleepless nights of watching over her old friend in the home they shared, with nurses at the bedside, her faithful companion of thirty-eight years

Rand Brooks as Charles Hamilton.

died. The next day at the studio she fought back tears and went through with her comedic scenes. When the director called for action continuing the reconstruction scenes after the Civil War, life, Miss Crews and *GWTW* went on uninterrupted.

He gave Marilyn Monroe her first screen kiss (*Ladies of the Chorus*) and played side-kick to Hopalong Cassidy, but it was as Scarlett O'Hara's

Butterfly McQueen (Prissy) and Vivien Leigh (Scarlett).

ill-fated first husband, Charles Hamilton, that Rand Brooks, at age twenty-one, earned screen immortality. He disliked the part of Melanie Hamilton's brother, preferring the more western macho roles. But he could not escape, even until his death at age eighty-four, the image of the young Confederate army soldier who died of measles, leaving Scarlett a not-so-inconsolable widow.

Who could forget Butterfly McQueen...portraying the slave girl "Prissy," who deceived Scarlett O'Hara into believing she could be counted upon to deliver Melanie's baby? And then when the time came, Prissy tearfully confessed, "I don't know nothin' 'bout birthin' babies, Miss Scarlett." Those lines kept Prissy's imitators, comics, and Butterfly's names before the public for years. McQueen was born in Tampa, FL, the daughter of a stevedore and a domestic worker. Her mother brought her to

New York as a child, and she acquired her nickname from her part in a "Butterfly Ballet."

An old friend of mine who used to work on *The San Francisco Examiner*, John Stark, met Butterfly (at the age of 75) while doing an article for *People* magazine. He described her then as short and stout, like a teapot, with closely-cropped gray hair and long metallic blue fingernails. "I was an only child," she told him. She never married, but is independent. She was paid a then respectable $5,000 for *GWTW*. "I support myself now from my actor's Equity pension, my social security and the rent I get from a house I own in Georgia." In 1980 she sued Greyhound Bus Lines for $300,000, after claiming she had been falsely arrested in the downtown Washington D.C. bus terminal and accused of being a pickpocket. In an out-of-court settlement, she received $60,000. Her home was in a studio in Harlem.

On December 23, 1995, Butterfly died after suffering critical burns when a kerosene heater caught fire. She was 84. Ms. McQueen was lying on the sidewalk when the Augusta Georgia firefighters arrived at her one bedroom cottage, which was destroyed. Her neighbors said McQueen had more than enough money to install central heating, but she flatly refused to do so. When firemen went through her papers after the fire, they found six signed checks to charities dated December 31, 1995. At the 50th anniversary of *GWTW*'s Atlanta premiere on December 15, 1989, Butterfly received the loudest applause as surviving cast members were introduced.

CHAPTER FOUR
VOICES

The writer's loft at the Selznick studios had a row of offices from which one could hear different voices with decidedly different accents. The most powerful of all was New York Jewish David O. Selznick's, Brooklyn's Ben Hecht, and New England's Sidney Howard. "The movie matches the novel almost scene for scene with illiterateness that not even Shakespeare or Dickens were accorded in Hollywood," wrote Frank S. Nugent of *The New York Times*.

"I find this studio the pleasantest studio that I have worked in," said F. Scott Fitzgerald. The Rolls-Royce of studios, Selznick International had gone through many name changes since it was built in 1918 and before Selznick took over in 1935. The main administration building was an exact replica of George Washington's home in Mount Vernon, Virginia. A classical colonnaded Southern-style mansion, it appeared to have been waiting for its part in *GWTW*. It is not too far off to say it had a human quality, compared to most factory-like studios around town. This quality permeated the sound stages of *GWTW* and their some 500 employees. There was a tremendous 'esprit de corps'. Eric's scrapbook was a testimony to all the activities that he organized. The S.I.P. Club (Selznick International Pictures) led by its president Eric Stacey met twice a month. There were parties, picnics and dances, besides inter-club sports games. After a picture was completed, a club party was given on one of the sound stages to which the entire cast was invited. Eric promoted everything to do with the filming, including social life and good fellowship. He loved a good time, had a great sense of humor, as you can see from the many photographs taken of Eric with the cast and crew, with his wry quips printed underneath.

The various departments of the Selznick studios were housed in separate cottages scattered about the lot. All were painted white, with shrubs against the walls, hedges lining the walkways and window boxes bright with flowers. The interiors were furnished like homes, with soft rugs, drapes, sofas and comfortable chairs. Towering over the cottages were numerous sound stages built of steel and concrete. The occupants of the cottages included Bill Menzies, head of the art department, Monty Westmore, the head make-up man, Harold Coles, head of the property department, Eddie Boyle head set-dresser and so on. Coles of property, and Boyle of set-dressing, were like two detectives as they went snooping around for props. Everything was a prop to them — even the sun and the moon. When Wilbur Kurtz *[Author's note: In the credits, Kurtz is listed as*

David O. Selznick in front seat.

"historian."] consulted them regarding his needs, you'd never know what they might bring back. They even found some rare mules, of the long-eared Georgia variety, for some of the opening scenes in the cotton fields. For the first time in motion pictures, a unique institution of ante-bellum days — the old cotton press — would make its appearance on the screen. The press was constructed in the carpenters shop at Selznick International,

Photographs of Eric Stacey with the cast and crew, with his own wry quips printed underneath.

according to exact measurements from plans drawn by Wilbur Kurtz. In the summer of 1922, Kurtz and his wife found an old cotton press, all parts still intact, though leaning to one side. The press was found on the Ellison plantation in Ellerslie, Georgia. Kurtz climbed all over the tipsy monster, taking measurements, dictating to his wife all sorts of figures, which she put down in a notebook. He made sketches of every detail and from these measurements, figures and sketches was able to make working drawings from which the *GWTW* cotton press was to be constructed. The ante-bellum cotton press was a thing of the past. It had gone the way of the old covered bridge, the well-sweep, and the water-wheel. In *GWTW* it would rise again. The final selection of carriages was made on sound stage 14. These old carriages are now museum pieces and with the advent of the movies early in the century, enterprising dealers began buying them up. Today, no purveyor of four-legged and four-wheeled props is without ample stable room and huge sheds to house these vehicles and their horse-power from a vanished civilization. For when all of the carriages have finally passed into oblivion, the musty ledgers of museum files and some few films may well constitute the only source material.

The production staff hard at work and all departments at the ready, the elusive screen-play lurched along with constant revisions. With casting problems resolved, screenwriter Ben Hecht, who had never liked Hollywood and saw in it only a source of quick money, was hired. Selznick was good under pressure and at work on *GWTW*, never having read it. He claimed that reading the book would only confuse him. Hecht worked without credit, writing at top speed after the original script was discarded by Selznick and the million-dollar cast was immobilized to the tune of $50,000 a day (1939 money). Hecht described the experience, "Twenty-four hour work shifts were quite common under David's baton. David himself sometimes failed to go to bed several nights in a row. He preferred to wait until he collapsed on his office couch. Medication was often necessary to revive him." Ultimately a pool of writers collaborated on the epic Civil War film.

The master script by Sidney Howard was considered just an agenda for rewrite teams and had been worked over in varying degrees by as many as ten hand-picked writers. He pushed his writers hard, staying up some nights all night, assisted by large doses of Benzedrine, thyroid tablets and sleeping pills. The uppers and downers played havoc with his disposition.

The writers had their personal problems to contend with, in addition to dealing with Selznick. Sidney Howard, for one, refused to work at the studio, extricating himself 3,000 miles away to his farm in Tyringham,

Massachusetts. He had all the clout to challenge Selznick, not only with his proven record of a string of successes but a Pulitzer Prize to back that up. The 46-year-old screenwriter from Oakland, California could not escape the blizzard of memos that descended on his bucolic retreat like a New England winter. Still, there were rare visits to Hollywood to confer with Selznick.

One writer interested Margaret Mitchell more than any other — novelist, short-story writer, and spokesman for the Jazz Age in the 1920s F. Scott Fitzgerald. An idol to flapper Peggy Mitchell, Fitzgerald's works dealt with the frenetic life style of the post World War I generation and the spiritual bankruptcy of the so-called American dream. His writings mirrored much of his own life, and the moral weaknesses, which pervaded the ruthless society of the 1920s. His last years as a scriptwriter in Hollywood were a desperate attempt to satisfy his and his even-more-neurotic wife, Zelda's, need for wealth and sensation after his crack-up at an early age following a success he was unable to handle, and his failure to develop as an artist.

When M-G-M fired Fitzgerald because of his excessive dependence on alcohol, he went directly to Selznick and landed a job on *GWTW*. The producer already had his script, but as was his custom he couldn't leave it alone. Rewriting would continue right up to the moment a shot was filmed (and printed). As Fitzgerald later wrote Maxwell Perkins, his editor and mentor at Scribner's, (known as the editor of genius-discoverer of Thomas Wolfe, Ernest Hemingway and Fitzgerald), "In *GWTW* I was absolutely forbidden to use any words except those of Margaret Mitchell. That is, when new phases had to be invented, one had to thumb through as if it were Scripture and check out phases of hers which would cover the situation." He spent several weeks on what he called "The Wind."

Meanwhile Mitchell wrote from Atlanta to Susan Myrick, a close friend whom she had recommended to Selznick as advisor in authenticating all manner of proper Southern dialect, background and character, as she was an expert in academe; "I'd wish you'd write something about Scott Fitzgerald when you get time. If anyone had told me ten or more years ago that he would be working on a book of mine I would have been stricken speechless. 'This Side of Paradise' is the most perfect crystallization of an era in all American fiction. It makes me feel sad when I think of how utterly past that era is now." She wrote her Georgian friend how she and her mother picked up the esthetic looking Scott in their car one day in 1918. They would haul up to twelve soldiers to town on occasion, when Fitzgerald was stationed at Camp Gordon near Atlanta during the war. At the time, she was deeply influenced by the literary and moral revolution of the 1920s, typified by F. Scott Fitzgerald.

Hand written samples of dialogue of Fitzgerald's from his *GWTW* working script, and various other pages, all signed by him, remain alongside those of David O. Selznick's notes in the archives at the University of Texas.

On a Thursday, January 26th, 1939 when *GWTW* actually started filming, as a friendly gesture to the success of the coming depiction of embattled Georgia, a luncheon was given by the Assistance League of Los Angeles, an organization similar to the Junior League. Three hundred guests were invited to pass through the beautiful Colonial entrance of the Selznick studios, some giving a salute to the confederate flag which had been raised .The waitresses were debutantes, sub-debs and minor film stars, who all donated their time. The proceeds of the luncheon were to go to charity. The program was dedicated to the old south and, with their faces blackened, the waitresses were dressed in gingham, white aprons and bandanas as they trekked up and down between the tables to the tune of southern music. The tables were covered with red and white covered checkered cloths, the central decoration being bowls of artificial cotton. Everything was southern down to the fried chicken — disjointed a la Dixie, of course-with all the trimmings. For a final touch, a pianist played "Dixie" and everyone rose. Truly, the south had risen again — in Hollywood.

The piece de resistance was the set for the city of Atlanta. Tara was also built on the back lot, though a few scenes were shot on location in the San Fernando Valley and Chico, California.. The recreated 'City of Atlanta' was the largest set ever built up to that time, consisting of 53 full-size buildings and 7,000 feet of streets. The reconstructed Peachtree Street alone was 3,000 feet long. (The amount of lumber that went into the sets, which were almost entirely facades, was roughly estimated at a million feet as estimated in Eric Stacy's diaries.)

GEORGE CUKOR

After much rehearsal, two scenes were set to be filmed on soundstage #3. Performers, cameras, lights and other equipment were all in place, and the crew moved about quietly and efficiently, with Eric Stacey overseeing. When Eric called 'quiet' — 'speed,' followed by a louder 'camera,' the temperature seemed to rise as the tension built. No coughing or stumbling

over wires or props now or they would have to do it all over again. When
the action began it was the only point of focus, as actors and onlookers
alike seemed to lose themselves in the moment. It was Scarlett's scene
on the steps of Tara. The huge boxy cameras were moving in on Scarlett,
fetchingly attired in the now legendary green sprigged muslin dress.

In the charity Bazaar scene, 10,000 articles of home manufacture,
most of them genuinely antique, were offered for sale. Rare cameos were
brought in the U.S. and Europe to be used on Scarlett's dresses; nothing
was overlooked to assure absolute realism. George Cukor was directing. He was here, there and everywhere — acting out the scene himself
with the cast. There were takes and re-takes, all kinds of adjustments. It
seemed endless and wearying. Cukor's patience was enviable. Gable's was
not. Cukor was demonstrating to Gable how to dance with more 'grace-
tempo-gaiety.' To Gable, rather unmanly. In any event Gable walked off
the set, leaving Vivien standing at the end of the line for the Virginia
Reel without a partner and wondering what had upset him. This was also
to be the last scene George Cukor directed on the picture. At six o'clock
that evening Cukor was still smiling and cheerful — an inspiration to cast
and crew. Vivien loved him. Gable remained skeptical. He took his prob-
lem home to talk over with Carole, who once confided to Jean Garceau,
"Clark isn't the happy-go-lucky man the public sees. He's not had a very
happy life and is inclined to be depressed and worried. I want to make it
up to him if I can and you've got to help me. Let's keep the gags going
and get him to relax and be happy." She told her agent, Myron Selznick,
that she would only do a film when Clark was working. Time with him
was so precious to her.

On Monday, February 13, in the midst of his myriad duties, director Cukor suddenly left the production. Much has been written about
this departure and who really might be to blame. However, behind the
scenes was the "King" (so called when columnist Ed Sullivan conducted
a poll among his readers and Gable won the title "King of Hollywood."
Number one at the box office for years over rival stars by an overwhelming
margin). King Gable's growing discontent with Cukor accelerated. Gable
knew that Cukor was gay and felt uneasy around him. He didn't mind
the discreet "gay couples," who were friends of his wife, but abhorred the
more obvious and promiscuous homosexuals who made him uncomfort-
able. While Cukor did not fall into this category, Gable evidently was not
able to separate his professional and personal feelings. It was probably
no accident that it was his idol, Victor Fleming, who took over where
Cukor left off. Apart from the fact that Cukor and Selznick had their

problems, no matter what Selznick may have thought of his old friend Cukor, it was clearly much more expeditious to change the director than to change a leading man who had been in the Top Ten at the Box-Office cash registers since 1932. The publicity alone would have been horrendous, let alone the expense.

Ann Rutherford, who played the youngest O'Hara daughter, recalled her days at M-G-M, "Clark Gable was the warmest, best-liked person on the set. He was adored by everyone who came in contact with him." This was corroborated by Jean Garceau over and over again during our many conversations. Gable and Cukor — like oil and water — simply did not mix.

Of Cukor, Ann Rutherford said, "He was the finest, most sensitive director in all of Hollywood. He displayed his fine shadowy hand in all the memorable intimate scenes that have touched audiences. Cukor gave a year of his life to coaching Vivien Leigh. And I remember after the day's shooting was done Vivien and Olivia would get into the car and drive to his house so he could coach them. That was after he had been replaced as director. It was Clark Gable who complained that George was not a man's director. Fleming (who replaced Cukor) was okay for the big war scenes, but he never had the sensitivity or patience for women's scenes." Rutherford, the daughter of former Metropolitan Opera tenor John G. Gilbert and of actress mother Lucille Mansfield, made her stage debut at the age of five. In 1937 she moved to M-G-M from Mascot Republic Pictures, where she gained popularity in the role of Polly Benedict, Mickey Rooney's ever-faithful girl friend in the 'Andy Hardy' series.

Gable, a man's man, loved outdoor sports, fishing and hunting, and could not relate to the sort of person Louella Parsons was describing when she said, "When I was talking to George on the phone one day I heard him scream — a mouse had run over his foot!" Cukor publicly addressed Gable on the set as 'Clark, dear/or honey,' and was known to enjoy gossip (one of the mainstreams of communication in Hollywood). He enjoyed good style and the repartee of intellectual stimulation. There is no doubt that 'honey' and 'dear' were generic expressions and in no way specific or personal — as anyone even remotely connected with the performing arts will know. Gable did not wish to differentiate. In retrospect, it may have been more Gable's inflexibility than Cukor's personality. It's hard to imagine that Cukor could have survived such a long and distinguished career on little more than good connections and a tart tongue. This is worth underscoring as Cukor would be vindicated by his many supporters in the industry, to Gable's lifetime regret, at the 1939 Academy Award presentations.

Selznick found Cukor's replacement on the set of *The Wizard of Oz*. Victor Fleming had three weeks remaining to complete direction of that film and L. B. Mayer immediately released him to his son-in-law David. Mayer had a lot to gain. Not only had he loaned Gable for *GWTW*, but the film would be released through his studio. While Gable was relieved to have his buddy Fleming on the set, Vivien wept to see Cukor leave, maintaining a strong friendship with him to her dying day. Fleming from Pasadena, California entered films as a cameraman in 1910, at age seventeen. He was a contemporary and pal of director Henry Hathaway, who directed his buddy John Wayne to an Oscar in *True Grit*. "Every dame he ever worked with fell on her ass for him," said Hathaway to me in his Bel-Air office, "in his usual uncompromising style." Six feet tall, great build, steel grey eyes, silvery hair and a deep voice conquered all. Gable owed everything he was, his personality to Vic. He modeled himself on him. When Gable said *GWTW* called for a man, not a flaming faggot, this was his idol Vic Fleming. Fleming, in his personal life, had a hot affair with Norma Shearer. His sexual talents were well publicized. When he directed *It* and *Mantrap* with Clara Bow he was caught in the Brooklyn redhead's love-net. In 1948 he had an affair with Ingrid Bergman. At age 56 Fleming now gave the orders on the set of *GWTW*— but not without the voice of Selznick trumpeting in his ear. The mood lightened somewhat on February 28. It was Wilbur Kurtz's birthday. Kurtz, an expert in Southern history, was a friend of Margaret Mitchell's. The studio decided to give him a party in the commissary, the studio's cafeteria restaurant.

On March 8, 1939 during the filming, after years of haggling, Gable got his divorce from his former wife Ria. He was now free to marry Carole Lombard, leaving at 4 a.m. on Wednesday, March 29th, the first two-day break in his schedule. Wearing old clothes to avoid being recognized, they drove 350 miles to Kingman, a small town in Arizona. When they arrived at the Marriage License Bureau, the clerk recognized them immediately and was so excited she could barely complete the forms. Jean Garceau laughed when she told me the story. Carole and Clark changed into their wedding clothes, married in a simple ceremony after a four-year relationship, with the minister's wife and her neighbor as witnesses. It was Gable's third and Carole's second marriage. The newlyweds returned to Hollywood that same night. The next day Gable went back to work on the picture — walking on air — and Jean Garceau and Carole returned to the ranch. Prior to their wedding, Clark and Carole had seen a house in Encino, in the San Fernando Valley area of Los Angeles, that they had fallen in love with. The two-story white brick and frame house with

its tall brick chimneys and dark green shutters resembled a Connecticut farmhouse. No swimming pool, tennis court or movie theatre, but a
small stable, a barn and chicken coops on 20 acres. Twelve miles from
Hollywood, it was a 45-minute drive to their studios.

As Gable sat in the kitchen in a captain's chair, elbows on the long
tavern table, looking out at the multi-colored flowers in the flowerpots on
the patio, he was deliriously happy. "It will be the first home that I've had
since I was a boy that I can really call my own." Gable always had a good
disposition in this environment while Carole was her characteristically
talkative, high-strung self.

CHAPTER FIVE

SHADOWS

When you're in love with a movie,
you grope for shadows that vanish at first touch.
The years lengthen, memories grow vague.

Ten days later, on Tuesday, March 28, 1939, at Selznick International in the cool gray dawn of a California morning, it was time to film Ashley's arrival scene on his return to Atlanta from the war at Christmas time. Set in December 1863, at the old car shed, it was to be filmed at the studio. It was quite a contrast to the beautiful sunny setting at Busch Gardens where the barbeque sequence was filmed. The barbecue had been a happy day in springtime before the war, whereas Ashley's homecoming, in mid-winter after three years of war, was overcast and sad. The car shed was an exact replica of the one that had stood in Atlanta from 1854 to 1864, and was built according to the original plans supplied by Wilbur Kurtz. Today, the blocks around the old railroad station in downtown Jonesboro have changed little and a number of plantation homes outside of town have also survived fairly well. Likewise, still in Jonesboro is the old county jail at King and McDonough Street, built in 1869 to replace yet another casualty of the war of E. A. Vincent, the architect. *[Author's note: The car shed, of course, was located in Atlanta. I'm confused by the sudden introduction of the railroad station in Jonesboro.]* During the hospital scenes it was thought advisable to attempt to locate a bona-fide physician of the 1860's to act as technical advisor. Unbelievably, one was found who had practiced medicine during the 1860's but he told them he did not think he could get away to come to the studio. He was assured that all arrangements would be made for his comfort, to which the 96-year-old doctor replied that he could get to the studio on his own all right but that he would not leave his patients.

Just weeks later the pressure of *GWTW* and Selznick's interference finally got to Victor Fleming, who turned prima donna himself, storming off the set and refusing to come back, claiming he'd had a nervous break-down. He even threatened to drive himself off a cliff. And Clark Gable was in complete sympathy with his macho counterpart. There had been tense moments between Fleming and Vivien leading up to his departure. His temper often got the better of him when she asked for guidance in playing her character when a scene was not as good as her impression of the one in the book. "Miss Leigh," he shouted, "you can take this script and stick it up your royal British ass." She needed his help, as sometimes she had to play four different ages in one day to accommodate the sets. Then there were the endless 'blue pages' of rewrites they kept getting on the set daily. Yet she persisted, especially when her behavior in a scene lacked logic. "What do I do here?" she asked. He replied curtly, "Ham it up!" as he did to Prissy. In spite of himself, Fleming admired her courage; and her work finally gained his greatest respect. By the end of shooting he was even becoming quite affectionate toward her. But Olivier stood in the way. How he handled her refusal to continue the love scenes between her and Gable unless Gable remedied the foul odor produced by his dentures and whiskey breath (she herself was impeccable with her hygiene) remained to be seen. Before he ran away, Fleming would often announce to his cast that they would 'only' have to complete three days work in an evening's shooting. Yet, he was the one to collapse under the strain. To replace Fleming — however temporarily — Selznick's father-in-law again came to the rescue. Sam Wood, director of M-G-M's *Goodbye, Mr. Chips*, moonlighted between the two studios.

Wood, 56, was a reliable craftsman who could turn even mediocre material into acceptable entertainment. His epic *Kings Row* was just three years ahead of him. *Goodbye, Mr. Chips*, the story of a lovable schoolteacher who ages from 25 to 83, starring British matinee idol Robert Donat and then new actress Greer Garson, would eventually be in competition with *GWTW* (particularly Mr. Chips versus Rhett Butler).

To lure Victor Fleming back took two weeks and a cage of lovebirds delivered to his Malibu Beach house by Vivien, Gable and Selznick — and possibly word of Sam Wood's good work to date on the picture, while he was absent was not unchallenging to his ego either. However, filming continued throughout April and May, with script changes handed out daily. At night the lot was often flooded with light. Peachtree Street, where Luckie Street joins, was never so bright — even when Sherman's torch spread its destruction northward from Five Points — that November night in 1864. A feeling of ghostly unreality came over those who viewed this reproduction of Atlanta's yesterday. An interesting part of all were the Green men who would move entire trees if necessary to produce the results drawn up by the graphic artists, whose composition was kept mindful of the cameraman and his crew. One night, Olivia de Havilland, preparing for the scene where she, as Melanie, and Scarlett are shown coming out of the hospital. They strolled around during breaks in filming, laughing, belying the otherwise ethereal look of Melanie. Errol Flynn, a strong Rhett Butler contender, adored this brown-eyed beauty, on screen and off.

Olivia de Havilland was born in Tokyo, the daughter of British patent attorney Walter de Havilland and Lillian Randolph, on July 1, 1916. She

Olivia de Havilland.

was brought to California at age three by her mother, after her parent's divorce, along with her younger sister Joan Fontaine. Although Olivia received a scholarship to Mills College, she never went. Stage struck, she appeared as Hermia in *A Midsummer's Night Dream*, both on stage at the Hollywood Bowl and in the 1935 screen version for Warner Bros. Her performance earned her a contract at Warner's and now she was on loan to Selznick for *GWTW*. Gable enjoyed Olivia's humor, and as he lived at home with a prankster, Carole, he had to have his little jokes at work, too. During rehearsal of a scene in which he, Rhett, takes Melanie in his arms down the steps of Aunt Pitty's house, after she had given birth, a dummy was used. On one occasion, having tenderly and gently carried the Melanie dummy to the wagon — and now being out of camera range, he unceremoniously dumped the bundle with a thump to the floor of the wagon, brushed his hands together and grinned at everybody. One particular night the cast and crew had to face the chill Pacific winds until 3:00 a.m. to film the harrowing departure sequence from Atlanta. Rhett, Scarlett, Prissy and Melanie's baby in the arms of his mother, were all piled into the old wagon being pulled by a frightened horse. This was the sequence leading up to the pyrotechnic scenes of the ammunition train explosion in the railroad yard. The horse lumbered through the debris littering the lower reaches of Peachtree Street, urged along by a determined Rhett. (This was a continuation of the very first take on December 10th when stunt doubles filled in for Gable and the unknown Scarlett.)

The cold night stimulated the appetite of the cast and crew, and supper was cooked on outdoor stoves and served cafeteria style. Turkey ala king on toast, coffee, sausages, rolls, string beans, potato salad, fruit and cookies were very much appreciated by everyone present. The extras had built a wood fire in the stove on a set of a grocery store! These extras, soldiers with torn, ill-fitting uniforms, bandaged and scarred, exchanged stories of their acting experiences on other films. The new relief director, Sam Wood, was on the job for the first time that night. Fleming had worked until 6p.m. and Woods took over at 7p.m. Wood would carry on until Fleming was rested and ready to return to work. Nothing, nor no one, would be allowed to stop production at this point. While all three units were at work on *GWTW*, there was one on location in Chico, taking long shots of outdoor farm scenes, another on the 40 acres, for exteriors, the third on the stage sets.

Britain's Royal Family had inadvertently given some unexpected publicity to *GWTW*, pleasing publicist Russell Birdwell immensely. In the Illustrated London News of May 13, 1939, there is a photograph of King

George VI and Queen Elizabeth taken on May 4th, two days before the royal couple sailed from Southampton on their visits to Canada and the U.S. The occasion was a dinner given at the American Embassy by Ambassador and Mrs. Joseph P. Kennedy. In the caption under the photograph of King George VI and Queen Elizabeth it noted that, "An all American menu was provided, including such specialties as mousse of Virginia ham and Uncle Sam savory." In the photograph the Queen is wearing a lovely gown designed along the lines of costumes of the 1860's. Queen Elizabeth was very much ahead of the coming Scarlett vogue, based on the charm and style of the costumes worn in the motion picture, and remained an arbiter of fashion until the day she died.

Twilight ushered in another night of work as preparations were made for a shot the coming Saturday, May 20th. This scene was to be a high point in the filming, so far as technical direction and the spectacular were concerned. This scene, many felt, was the most memorable in the movie. Scarlett, having left Melanie at home in labor in the care of Prissy, marked her way through hundreds of wounded soldiers outside the train station looking for Dr. Meade, whom she must bring back to Aunt Pittypat's to deliver the baby. This was to be Selznick's panoramic spectacle, a composition of every available extra — he wanted 2,000, but he could only get 800. So, he decided to use dummies to fill in. The Screen Extra's Guild however insisted that the dummies be paid the same wages for their inclusion in the scene. Selznick rightfully refused! On that day 800 extras, clothed by wardrobe in bloody tattered uniforms, lay groaning in the sun, each man manipulating a soldier-dummy at his side.

Normally, the cameras would be mounted on dollies or tripods, but this time the largest crane on the West Coast was called for. To capture the effect they were seeking, this special crane was used to lift the camera high into the air. The boom, 85 feet in length would move the camera from dead level to a 45-degree angle. The cameraman and directors were to be suspended on a platform from the boom. This would give the angle and depth for the imposing pullback shot, where Scarlett crosses the railroad yards looking for Dr. Meade, threading her weary way through more and more bodies as the camera draws higher and higher and further away until there were 1,888 figures in camera range — wounded soldiers evacuated from the battle of Jonesboro. The arched facade of the car shed framed the view on the left: the stores, offices and the hotels of wartime Atlanta on the right. In the left hand corner, the war-torn Confederate flag was still flying pathetically in the wind, as the multiple horrors of war were displayed for the camera in an unfolding orgy of misery, tragedy and defeat.

Eric Stacey bellowed instructions through his megaphone as director Fleming briefed a tense Vivien Leigh just prior to filming the great
pullback shot of the wounded soldiers at the train station. Soon, Fleming,
Stacey, and the camera crew rode high above the ground on the camera
platform as it made a rehearsal pass over the railroad yard and the confederate flag; the crane lifting them to its maximum height. Vivien, as

Vivien after Battle of Atlanta, waiting for her cue.

Scarlett, waited for her cue looking exhausted and almost defeated —
perfect for the scene to come.

On the Peachtree Street set, she stood on the porch of the Atlanta
Hotel waiting for her next shot. In this scene she was to leave the hospital
en route to Aunt Pitty's house while the siege of Atlanta was in progress.
Eric Stacey and Fleming were ready to shoot the sequence where Scarlett
ran recklessly through the congestion on Peachtree Street, dodging horses,
wagons, and ambulances, in her race to get back to her Aunt's house,
where Melanie lay in labor, and unable to take any more of the horrors
of the hospital; the sickness of the dying men. She was fleeing to join the
further havoc and congestion of the evacuating citizenry. Now, this scene
was extremely dangerous to shoot. It terrified the horses, no doubt made
some of those present more than a little concerned for Miss Leigh. Clark

Gable (on his day off) came to the set to watch, knowing the importance of the shot to be filmed — but mainly to observe the feisty little Miss Leigh go through her paces so daringly. A tired looking Vivien sat in a canvas folding chair between takes, waiting for the sets to be re-set. So affected was she by the Civil War book and what this action meant that she was like a general going into Battle, totally aware of the strategy

Eric on boom surveying the next scene.

required to win in the fray. Robert E. Lee could have used her cunning in his defense against Grant. Vivien refused the use of a double for this: "The sequence could not be done all in one continuous take," she recalled, "and so for what seemed like an eternity I dodged through the maze of traffic on Peachtree Street timing myself to avoid galloping horses and thundering wagons…and between each shot, the make-up man — he

Vivien Leigh (Scarlett) and Harry Davenport (Dr. Meade).

seemed to be everywhere at once — came running to wash my face, then dirty it up again to just the right shade of Georgia clay dust. I think he washed my face about 20 times in one day — and dusted me over with red dust after each washing. Here, of course, was where the tremendous task of organization was at its most spectacular. Horses and riders had to cross certain places at just the right time — and so did I."

Often it had to be so accurate that a small stone or cross taped on the street marked precise spots where she must be for the camera, often at split-second timing — and provided she would not meet oncoming galloping horses or a wagon out of position and headed for the same spot. Men who towered over the diminutive Vivien showed the strain of the effort required to capture this scene, while she stood hands on hips, poised and ready for another take. Everyone was astonished at her courage and fortitude. Electricians, grips, make-up men and carpenters stood around and watched take after take, breaking into spontaneous applause after Vivien had played the highlights in her most dramatic scenes, "You'd know you had something as they are the world's severest critics," said Gable, who led the applause. Vivien said, "In fact I was so intent on being in the right place at the right time all day that I did not realize until I got to bed that night that Scarlett O'Hara Leigh was a badly-bruised person."

There was always more to come for Scarlett O'Leigh! A dressing room trailer and a convoy of trucks were used to transport cast, crew and equipment to Lasky Mesa, in the Simi Valley (sixty miles from the studio) to film what many feel is the most powerful scene — out of so many to choose from — in the picture. *[Author's Note: Jesse Lasky, Jr. told me, during one of our meetings, that Lasky Mesa was so named because some of his father's early films were shot there in the very primordial days of Hollywood.]*

On Tuesday, May 23rd, at 11 p.m., they left the studio once again, following a full day's shooting, for the drive north to Lasky Mesa to try to capture the perfect dawn on film. Vivien, subjected to a grueling schedule as it was, only asked for longer workdays to complete her scenes so that she could join Olivier in New York, where he was rehearsing *No Time For Comedy* scheduled to open on Broadway on April 17, 1939.

To replicate as near as possible what Margaret Mitchell had described as "of savagely red land — blood colored after rains, brick dust in droughts, the best cotton land in the world" — in other words the red clay of North Georgia. In the movie the plain brown dirt of the San Fernando Valley was specially tinted red for the outdoor shots. The sunrise had to be cinematically perfect, without cloud formation and without the possibility of any clouds drifting into camera range. Vivien climbed to her position on the hillside silhouetted against the sunrise.

Suffering from hunger after the war, Scarlett's memory would often return to the meals served of the old days: the candle-lit table, food fragrances perfuming the air, rolls, corn muffins, biscuits and waffles dripping butter, all at one meal. Ham at one end of the table and fried chicken at the other, collards swimming in rich port liquor iridescent with grease, snap beans in mountains on brightly flowered porcelain, fried squash, stewed okra, carrots in cream sauce thick enough to cut. And three desserts, chocolate cake, vanilla blancmange and pound cake topped with sweet whipped cream. It was probably just such memories, when hunger gnawed at her empty stomach, that caused Scarlett to raise her hand heavenward and cry to God, "...I'll never be hungry again." Eric Stacy's scrapbook contained a Call Sheet for this location shooting in Tara's vegetable garden. In this scene, where Scarlett gags on a radish, Vivien refused to make wrenching noises and Olivia de Havilland offered to dub them in for her.

```
                    SELZNICK INTERNATIONAL

                         presents




               "G O N E   W I T H   T H E   W I N D"


                       from the novel by

                      MARGARET MITCHELL




                          starring

                        CLARK GABLE

                        VIVIEN LEIGH

                        LESLIE HOWARD

                    OLIVIA DE HAVILLAND



    Final Shooting Script              Screen Play by
    January 24, 1939.                  SIDNEY HOWARD

                                       Produced by
                                       DAVID O. SELZNICK

                                       Directed by
                                       VICTOR FLEMING
```

Opening page from the script.

Selznick-International Pictures — Call Sheet
Date May 23, 1939 — Tuesday
Summer 1864 (Weather Permitting)
Scenes SC. 383 (Dawn)
Vivien Leigh on Set 2:00 AM
Make-up 1:00AM
Later
Exterior – Tara Creek Bottom Cotton Patch Autumn 1864
Shooting script – page 125 – scene 314 long shot desolate fields

As Scarlett walks away from the camera toward the vegetable garden, which is on a knoll to the right, she passes the well, the ruined orchard, the cotton fields with only a few miserable patches of white remaining. In the background *(b.g.)* we see charred slave quarters and barn, the paddock, the scorched trees, the skeleton of the cotton press, and the ruins of the split-rail fence, which had been around the kitchen garden

Scene 315 – Close shot – Vegetable Garden – Ruined outhouses in background B.G.

The soft earth, scarred with hoof prints and heavy wheels — the vegetables mashed into the soil. Scarlett wearily comes into the garden and looks down at the earth, As she stoops to pick some radishes from a short row *(CAMERA PANS DOWN WITH HER)* she kneels and eats several as fast as she can get them into her mouth, not bothering to remove the dirt. Suddenly she gets ill to her stomach-and slowly, miserably she retches as she falls face forward on the ground and sobs.

(CAMERA HOLDS) on the portrait of the defeated, prostrate and sobbing figure, This is the lowest moment in Scarlett O'Hara's life — and we should feel that she is completely defeated. After we have held this portrait, the sobs slowly stop — and *(CAMERA MOVES DOWN)* to Scarlett's head. Her head moves somewhat so that we can see her face — and we see her expression change slowly into bitter determination. Ever so slowly, and with grim determination, she pulls herself up on her hands and as *(CAMERA STARTS TO DRAW BACK)* she rises to one knee — and finally straightens up.

Page 126 Scene 315 – This is the crucial moment of Scarlett's O'Hara's life. And it is the most magnificent moment of her life. Out of this complete defeat a new and mature Scarlett O'Hara is born. She stands there, fist clenched, her dress soiled, faced smudged with dirt and speaks slowly with grim determination — measuring each phrase carefully. Before speaking she raises her clenched fist and looks up, delivering her speech to the sky:

Scarlett: "As God is my witness…as God is my witness…they're not going to lick me!…I'm going to live through this and when it's over I'll never be hungry again…no. nor any of my folks!…if I have to lie-steal-cheat — or kill! AS God is my witness, I'll never be hungry again." She stands, her fist still clenched, *(as CAMERA DRAWS BACK)* on the determined figure outlined against the devastation of the plantation.

Commenting on some of her work in the film and on that scene in particular, Vivien said, "Oddly enough, the scenes of physical strain were not so wearing as the emotional ones. Another night we worked at the Selznick Studios until about 11 o'clock, then went out to the country, once more, for a shot against the sunrise, when Scarlett falls to her knees in the run-down fields of Tara and vows she'll never be hungry again. We made the shot and when I arrived at home, I do not recall that I was so terribly tired. Instead, I think of the day that Scarlett shoots the deserter, and I recall that after that nerve-wracking episode, both Olivia, the wonderful Melanie of the film, and myself were on the verge of hysterics — not alone from the tenseness of the scene, but from the too realistic fall as the 'dead' man went down the stairs before us."

Gable had his memorable scenes as well. Jean Garceau and Carole went to Pasadena to watch the scene where Bonnie, Rhett's daughter, is thrown from her pony. Clark was fond of Cammie King, who played Bonnie, and brought her over to the ladies to introduce her, "This is my real sweetheart," and Carole pretended to be jealous and cry. Years later when Clark ran into Cammie in London, on her way to finishing school in Switzerland, she still greeted him as 'Father Rhett'. Cammie King Conlon's 's mother knew the casting director at Selznick Studios and she used her connections to get her little girl into the picture. Cammie's older sister, Diane, was originally set to play Bonnie, but by the time the movie was ready to start she had outgrown the part. *[Author's note: In Cammie's new book, she has a new "take" on this story.]* Her memories of her time on the set are sometimes vague, sometimes vivid. She does remember how kind Gable was to her and how distant the temperamental Vivien Leigh seemed, "I'm sure she hated me," Conlon said.

On June 27, 1939, five months after her first scene was shot, Vivien completed her last take on *GWTW*. Alone in her dressing room she ate a sandwich and a salad, cast an unregretful look at her worn copy

Scarlett keeping her pomise to 'never go hungry again!'

of Margaret Mitchell's novel and walked over to make up — and then onto a rehearsal set to test for *Rebecca.* The novel *Rebecca,* by Daphne du Maurier (published in 1938), is an impeccably-crafted Gothic love story about a shy, sensitive orphan who has been traveling about the continent as companion to an overbearing American social climber. The brooding Maxim de Winter sweeps the naive young woman off her feet, marries her and takes her to his country estate, Manderley, not realizing that the spirit of his late wife would insinuate her memory into their lives.

Vivien went valiantly through her test scenes but, for the first time, the ghost of "Scarlett" came between her and the part that she so desperately wanted, opposite her lover, Laurence Olivier, in much the same way that the ghost of Rebecca would come between the widowed Mr. de Winter and his un-named second wife.

Fade In: The cast and crew — at least those who had survived — with sighs of relief and tears of joy that they had actually made it through filming; somewhat wistful that it was now over (though not quite comprehending at that moment what was to be), looked forward to the usual end-of-shooting 'wrap party.' Once photographed, the life of Scarlett and Rhett was over for them, or so they believed. Yet *GWTW* will serve as David O. Selznick's masterwork for as long as there are projection machines and screens on which to show it. And millions of people around the world continue to take it to their hearts, creating a new icon of this spellbinding account of the passion and romance of two people set against the backdrop of the Civil War, giving them, and practically everything brushed by *GWTW*, an aura of immortality

The wrap-up party for *GWTW* was given on Stage #5, the set for Rhett Butler's mansion. The entire cast put in an appearance; and some of the crew, now off of Selznick's treadmill, cut loose and got drunk. Many photos were taken and a hand movie projector was given to property man Bill Clark, a friend to all, to take home movies of the party.

Eric's scrapbook contained six snapshots to a page and a sample page might include Carole Lombard in a full-length silver fox (in June) with her husband, Clark Gable and Victor Fleming in suits wearing matching ties, and Selznick and Vivien posed with almost everybody. Smiling though she was in every shot, Vivien found herself saddened as she said goodbye to the cast, the studio technicians, the crew, and all the others she knew she would not likely see again. There were exchanges of gifts and Selznick presented Vivien with a lighter in the shape of a star, as a memento of Scarlett — no doubt to signify the stardom which he was certain would be hers world-wide with the release of the film. The lighter was stolen in later years and, though her professional stardom was never in doubt, a deep shadow would eclipse her personal life.

While Vivien and Olivier talked over their future plans, including what she believed would certainly be her co-starring role in *Rebecca*. "Scarlett intervened." Here's a funny thing…, Vivien said, "We began actual work on the picture January 26th of 1939. The first scene was the same that the book opens with, where the Tarleton twins are on the porch talking to Scarlett. [One of the twins was George Reeves, later known as Superman to millions of TV fans. He fell in love with Leigh during the shot.] Then on the 26th of May it was found necessary to reshoot that scene for some technical reason." (For the re-shoot Selznick felt that Scarlett, at sixteen, would look more her age wearing a white dress instead of the more provocative flowered green one already filmed.)

And when David saw those rushes he exploded, when he ran into her in the corridor, "What on earth has happened to you? You look so different. My God you look old!"

"And so would you if you had been working eighteen hours a day for weeks on end," she snapped back. "The truth is I was so tired I did not look young anymore! Scarlett goes from sixteen to twenty-eight in the

Leigh in white dress.

picture and I looked all right for the later transitions. But we had to wait until October when I was rested again really, to get that opening sequence!" One look at Vivien's face was enough for Selznick to postpone any retakes until she had had enough time to rest. More importantly, he knew that her going to New York to be with Olivier would do her the most good. Olivier's father had died, and since he was leaving the play (*No Time For Comedy*), they planned to go to England.

In spite of what he knew must be her happiness at joining Olivier and going home, Selznick saw that she was crying. To answer his questioning look she explained, "Scarlett's dead. You see she's dead and we've been together so deeply."

"The hell she is! You two will go on forever," he retorted in a moment of prophecy. Then Vivien confessed, "I knew it was a marvelous part, but I never cared for Scarlett. I couldn't find anything of myself in her, except for one sentence. The odd thing is that they would cut it out in the various re-writing that went on, but I always fought to have it put back. It was the only thing in the character that I could take hold of. It's the scene after Frank's funeral (Scarlett's second husband) when Scarlett gets drunk and tells Rhett how glad she is that her mother is dead and can't see her. My mother brought me up to be kind and thoughtful and ladylike, just like her, and I've been such a disappointment. I liked Scarlett then for her honesty." Scarlett O'Hara's war ended on the 40 acres. For Vivien Leigh the war in Europe was about to begin, as letters from friends in England brought foreboding news.

The worldwide depression began with the New York stock market crash of 1929. Though conditions improved somewhat as the 1930's progressed, the Depression was never completely overcome. The past was resurrecting itself, with the usual political corruptions — only bigger and more widespread. It seems that those destined to live without political power during times of war and social upheaval become ever the victims — unable to find comfort in the past, peace in the present, or hope for the future.

Vivien, exhausted and without the driving force of her schedule, was longing to return to England, now that she was reunited with Olivier — but the part of Scarlett had claimed her psyche more than she realized. Olivia de Havilland told me that when she hadn't seen her for weeks, she actually didn't recognize her or sense her aura. "She had lost so much weight, looking demised by overwork, almost depleted. Her whole atmosphere had changed. She gave something to that film which I don't think she ever got back."

The Civil War on 40 acres ended on June 27, 1939. Six months later the United States would be dragged unwillingly into World War II. A chill wind blowing across Europe was soon to sweep across the Atlantic onto American shores. Escape became the solace of the masses as they sought to avoid having to deal with the depression and the oncoming conflagration, even if only temporarily. In 1939 moviegoers lined up to buy tickets at a rate of eighty million a week. And *GWTW* was undoubtedly the most eagerly awaited motion picture ever — a Gallup poll indicated that 56.6 million people were anxiously awaiting its release. Cut, edited and musically scored, *GWTW* was shown to a select private audience in Riverside, California; and it was evident that Selznick had created a masterpiece. Shining through came the towering performances of Clark Gable and Vivien Leigh. Gable's success with the role was widely anticipated; it was tailor made, even though his mouthful of blazing white teeth were false and his jug-handle ears had to be taped back, this was his pinnacle. With Vivien Leigh it was different. That final scene left the audience spellbound. Reading from Eric Stacy's script from Sidney Howard's screen play screen:

Final shooting script January 24, 1939 Scene 617 page 255:

Scarlett *(lifting her face)* "Tara! Home! I'll go home — and I'll think of some way to get him back." She lifts her chin higher. "After all, tomorrow is another day."

She was a revelation. A new star of unprecedented magic! Now she belonged to the world. It brought Selznick to the heights of the film industry at age thirty-seven, and, with *GWTW,* immortalizes the name of Selznick, vindicating his father's checkered past in the business.

He wanted to glorify his achievement. He alerted Russell Birdwell to add to the hysteria of *GWTW* with plans for its World Premier, in Atlanta on December 15, 1939, at the Lowe's Grand on Peachtree Street. Atlantans were delirious. It was to be a state holiday — a three-day celebration. The Mayor gave all civic employees and school children the day off. For this occasion, the South would rise again. In October, Vivien wrote her mother, who had returned to England, to tell her about the upcoming premiere. Gertrude Hartley wrote back, including news of wartime preparations in London, which unsettled Vivien. Practically everyone involved with the forthcoming gala was jubilant, though there were some exceptions. Ann Rutherford was thrilled to be going. Evelyn Keyes must go — after all; she was a native of Atlanta. Hattie McDaniel wanted to go but couldn't; Atlanta in the 1930s was still a segregated city. Victor Fleming was undecided, still sore at Selznick for even suggesting that he share directorial credits on the film with George Cukor and Sam Wood. Leslie Howard refused — England was at WAR! (He would soon leave Hollywood to join the cause) Olivia de Havilland was delighted to go. If Laurence Olivier was not to be invited then Vivien responded succinctly to her invitation — "David be fucked! I won't go." Margaret Mitchell wrote from Atlanta that she just wanted to run away. Of course not to have its author and star was intolerable to all involved. Margaret stayed on and Olivier packed his bags to accompany his lover.

Hitler's war in Europe would have to wait. The Civil War was back in a frenzy that occupied the City of Atlanta, though more important events were happening around the world. The Soviet Union was invading Finland, Nazi Germany was digesting Poland as storm clouds glowered over Europe, while little men strutted and postured across political landscapes. In 1939, Hollywood was having its most glorious year. A group of films appeared, the likes of which we never saw again: the burning sands of Fort Zinderneuf in *Beau Geste*, a Stage C headed for a rendezvous with the Ringo Kid in *Stagecoach*, Dorothy's trek toward the emerald city to see *The Wizard of Oz*, the tryst atop the Empire State Building in *Love Affair*, Heathcliff's spirit uniting with Cathy's on the moors of *Wuthering Heights*. Garbo laughed in *Ninotchka*, and the country cried as they said *Goodbye, Mr. Chips*. Heartbreak as Rhett left Scarlett, perhaps forever — now everything was *Gone With the Wind*.

Despite the segregation policies, the wonderful contributions of Hattie McDaniel, Butterfly Mc Queen, Oscar Polk, Everett Brown, and Eddie Anderson were not overlooked. Margaret Mitchell recognized Hattie in a personal way and sent her a set of Wedgwood cups and saucers, each saucer hand-painted with an Atlanta landmark of the Civil War Era. Selznick wrote, praising Hattie, "I should like at this time to congratulate and thank you for your brilliant performance as Mammy in *GWTW*. I think you will find it is universally acclaimed as one of the finest performances of this or any other year."

The premiere brought the Gables in from California in a chartered American Airlines plane with *GWTW* painted on its fuselage. The reluctant Gable had to be gently persuaded by Carole, "Listen, you fat-assed Dutchman, you're going! I'm not going to miss this!"

From here on out, the following details shall be omitted, having been so excruciatingly reported in several other *GWTW* books. One comment may be of interest however: Leslie Howard, having returned to England weeks before during a blackout in London, had been involved in an auto accident which left him with a fractured jaw, broken teeth and chest injuries. Sans Howard, the guest list read like America's commercial and social royalty: among them Rockefellers, Vanderbilts, Whitneys, McAdoos, Baileys, and Rickenbackers. Everyone wanted to be there at the 2,100 seat theatre, even the ambitious young pastor of Ebenezer Baptist Church. The Reverend Martin Luther King, Sr. arranged for his young choir to sing spirituals before the tuxedoed, totally-white audience. The choir came dressed as field hands.

The night before at the costume ball Vivien was the Belle of the Ball; while darkly-grinning Gable's head was in a whirl, surrounded by hundreds of pretty girls — one looked at him too long, gasped, "Lord, I can't stand this any longer," and fainted. At the end of the party, just before the screening, Rhett Butler met his creator. Though they had been born within three months of each other, at the turn of the century, Gable seemed more mature as he crooked his neck to gaze down at the 4'11" Mitchell, looking girlish in a big bowed hat. Margaret had said at one time that the role of Prissy was the only part she would have liked for herself.

Many years later when Jean Garceau reminisced, she laughed as she told me this story: Following the festivities, shortly after the Gables checked out of their suite at Atlanta's Georgian Terrace Hotel, Carole's hairdresser overheard a conversation at the front desk. A little old lady was asking for the room which had been occupied by Clark. The room clerk said it was available but there would be a slight delay while it was cleaned and the linen changed. "Now, are you sure it's the same room he had?" "Yes, of course," the clerk told her. "Then I'll take it right now," she said decisively," and don't change the sheets."

In London and all over Britain, *GWTW* achieved exceptional runs — and these were the war years. At the Empire and the adjoining Ritz Theatre it ran for 232 weeks — approximately 4-1/2 years, 24 weeks in Glasgow, and 17 in Birmingham, coinciding with the city's worst blitz.

On the night of February 29, 1940, at the world-famous Cocoanut Grove, *GWTW* took home ten Oscars. Of course Leigh won as best actress, while Gable, who should have won, did not. Robert Donat, "Mr. Chips," did, perhaps as chastisement for Gable's hand in the George Cukor firing. The ghost of Sidney Howard hovered over the festivities. Howard, who had been fatally run over by his tractor on his Massachusetts farm, became the first posthumous Oscar winner for his writing of the screen play. When Olivia de Havilland discovered that someone else had won for Best Supporting Actress, she ran to the ladies' room, crying. It was

Hattie McDaniel's name that was announced instead, and a loud "HAL-LELUJAH!" rang out from supports at the back of the room. McDaniel was elated for herself and her race because she was the very first black performer to win this award. Olivia later pulled herself together and congratulated Hattie. Scarlett O'Hara's father, Thomas Mitchell, won Best Supporting Actor — for *Stagecoach!* Mitchell was unforgettable in every

role he played. (Again, all of this has been well documented in other books).

As the Gables drove to the celebration party, Carole tried to cheer her husband up, "Aw, don't be blue, Pappy. We'll bring one home next year."

"No, we won't. This was it. This was my last chance. I'm never gonna go to one of these things again."

Carole spun around, "Not you, you self-centered bastard. I mean me!"

In December, 1940, the Gables went to John Hopkins Hospital in Baltimore for Clark to have a painful shoulder examined. During the filming of *San Francisco* in 1936, he had been buried

At the Academy Awards ceremony, 1940, when Vivien received her Oscar.

beneath a falling brick wall. Though the bricks were made of paper mache', the impact and cumulative weight of them had injured him and he was concerned about persistent discomfort. The doctors found nothing seriously wrong and recommended deep massage and exercise. Relieved at the news, the Gables went on to see the sights. When President Roosevelt heard they were in town, he invited them to the White House study while he delivered a Fireside Chat, on the radio.

On the morning of December 7, 1941, carrier-based Japanese aircraft slipped through the dawn into Pearl Harbor and America was at war. With the attack on Pearl Harbor, Hollywood plunged into the war wholeheartedly. On that first Sunday in December, Jean and Russ Garceau had just come home from church when they received a call from the Gables, telling them that Pearl Harbor had been bombed. Jean arrived at the office the next day to find Clark waiting to dictate a letter to President Roosevelt, offering Carole's and his services as they might be needed, and sent it off post haste.

Meanwhile, Carole received a request to launch Indiana's bond drive on January 15 in Indianapolis. (She was born in Ft. Wayne, Indiana.). Clark

Thomas Mitchell.

could not accompany her, go to Washington, and still be ready for his next picture, so he suggested that Carole's mother, Bessie, also a native Hoosier, accompany her. "I'll ask Otto (Otto Winkler their Press Relations representative) to go along — just to keep an eye on you dames." Jean so wanted to join the group. Although, she usually did not like to leave her husband and home, Carole explained, she saw Jean's disappointment. "Don't worry. When I get back we're going to New York. Pa and I will take you. We'll shop, see all the shows, and have a grand time." Carole had to leave the day before Clark returned from Washington. They had never been separated before for any length of time. Since she couldn't welcome him home, Carole wrote a series of notes, one for each day she would be gone, and asked Jean to give him one every morning. "Carole was not overly affectionate with her women friends; but when she was ready to leave, she hugged me hard, kissed me and said, 'Take care of my old man for me, will you, Jeanie?'"

The tour train made stops for station appearances, press interviews, and platform talks to support the bond campaign. Carole telephoned from Salt Lake and told Clark how surprised she was at the enormous crowd that had greeted her, despite ten-degrees-below-zero weather. The next call was from Ogden, Utah and then from Chicago. Thursday, January 15, the party arrived in Indianapolis. She had sold over two million dollars worth of bonds. The bond tour now concluded, Bessie and Winkler favored returning home by rail, but Carole said she couldn't bear three days by train, she was so anxious to get back to Gable. Bessie was very concerned about flying that day. A strong believer in numerology and astrology, she warned Carole and Winkler that it was January 16 and that the number 16 was a warning of possible accident or death. Moreover, she said, her astrologer had advised her just a few weeks before: "Stay off planes in 1942." Although Carole was also interested in astrology and usually followed her mother's advice, she insisted on returning home by airplane.

When they arrived at the Indianapolis airport, Bessie became further alarmed about flying that day when she learned that their flight number was 3, they would be flying on a DC-3 and furthermore, Carole was thirty-three years old.

Carole, Bessie, and Otto Winkler boarded a Douglas DC-3 airliner — TWA Flight #3, leaving Indianapolis at 4:00 p.m., which was scheduled to arrive in Burbank, California, that night after stops in Albuquerque, New Mexico, and Las Vegas, Nevada. Winkler wired Gable that the flight would arrive at 8:00 pm. Gable instructed the servants to plan and prepare a marvelous homecoming dinner. Joining them would be Carole's brothers, Winkler and his wife, Jill. Fresh flowers were placed everywhere throughout the ranch home. As a gag, Gable put a store window mannequin under the sheets of Carole's bed. The plane was later to be filled to capacity with airmen returning from the Army Ferrying Command to a base in California. A TWA employee asked Winkler if the Lombard party would relinquish their seats for three more army men. Carole chose not to. She was allowed to make this refusal because she was returning from a government war bond rally assignment. Flight #3 flew nonstop from Albuquerque to Burbank. This time however, it stopped in Las Vegas at 6:36 pm to refuel. At 7:07 p.m. it took off for Burbank.

Larry Barbier, an M-G-M publicist, had been sent to Burbank Airport to meet the party. He was to call Gable as soon as he had the exact arrival time. Gable had decided not to go to the airport, knowing photographers and reporters would be there to cover Carole's return, and he did not want to interfere. He waited at the ranch. The call from Barbier did not come. Instead a call came from Eddie Mannix, an M-G-M official and one of his closest friends. "Carole's plane went down a few minutes after it left Las Vegas," Mannix said somberly.

The plane crashed into Table Rock Mountain about thirty miles southeast of Las Vegas. Jean received a phone call from Clark at 8 p.m., saying that Carole's plane was down and he was going to the Burbank airport with Jill Winkler. He called again from the airport. He was taking a chartered flight directly there. In Las Vegas he went to the sheriff's office, where the men were planning a rescue mission. "How do you know the plane is there?" Clark asked. "Because it's on fire. The flames shot up two to three hundred feet." When the group started out, Clark wanted to go along, but was persuaded to wait in Vegas for news. When the men reached the wreck, they found that the heat of the flames had melted the snow and blackened the trees. A charred script found near a body and a wisp of un-scorched blond hair in the forward section of the fuselage identified Carole. A telegram sent to Gable read: "No survivors. All killed instantly." At 4 p.m. Clark called Jean. He said quietly, "Ma's gone."

CHAPTER SIX
GHOSTS

Clark spent hours roaming the ranch alone, watching Carole's films on the projector, and looking through scrapbooks of their life together, then drank himself to sleep. He stared blankly at the Dodge station wagon in the garage, remembering their trips together, and never drove it again. He told the household staff to leave Carole's room untouched, unchanged. Everything was to remain the way she left it. For months after her death, he was almost out of his mind with grief. He'd have dinner alone in the dining room with Carole's dog and cats near the table. Everywhere he looked there was a reminder of her.

Eerie sightings of Carole have been reported. Her ghostly form is said to have roamed the house! Lights flickered, candles snuffed out, faucets turned on and off, and doors suddenly opened and closed. One psychic, who had come to investigate, told the real estate broker that he saw her walking down the stairs in a long red gown, going to meet someone with dark hair.

Then, in the summer of 1942, at forty-one years of age, Clark Gable enlisted as a private in the United States Army. "I don't want to sell war bonds. I don't want to entertain. I just want to be where the going is tough!" He left Hollywood immediately upon finishing *Somewhere I'll Find You* and was off the screen for the next three years. He asked Jean to have the remains of Carole's ruby and diamond clip, found in the wreckage, put into a gold case, which he would wear around his neck together with his dog tags.

November 22, 1945, Thanksgiving Day — after six years of global slaughter — World War II was over and America's fighting men were streaming home. Grieving for those who had fallen, grateful for those who had survived, the nation that solemn autumn day gave thanks that peace had come at last. For the lucky ones who were there, the memories are rich and resonant.

Gable finally came to realize that *GWTW* had immortalized him and, after WWII, he confessed to Selznick, whom he never liked, that "The only thing that has kept me a big star has been the revivals of GWTW.

Every time the picture is re-released a whole new crop of young moviegoers gets interested in me."

The "king" of Hollywood 1930s confronted the "love goddess" of the
1950s. When she was born, he was twenty-six. When he made *GWTW,*
she was thirteen. In 1960, they collided to co-star in *The Misfits*. And they
were both played out by then.

Born Norma Jean Baker in Los Angeles, reared by twelve sets of foster
parents, she turned to acting to get noticed. As a 'love goddess' she starred
in thirty films that grossed more than $200 million. At various times, at
odds with her studio bosses, unhappy in her marriages, unable to find sat-
isfaction in her worldwide fame, she tried in precarious ways to escape the
pressures and false images created by her Hollywood publicity. She was
forever two people — a true Gemini — scared little Norma Jean whom
everyone wanted to protect, and glamorous Marilyn Monroe who played
around with a President. One part made us love her. The other part made
her a legend — after her death in 1962. When shooting began on *The
Misfits,* July 18, 1960, she had just turned thirty-four. At the beginning of
her first scene with Gable, she breathed, "Rhett Butler, to think I'm working with him!" Apart from that fact she showed little interest in *The Misfits*.

Soon after filming the calamitous *The Misfits,* Gable suffered a heart
attack. On November 6, 1960, he was rushed to Presbyterian Hospital
where he died ten days later, on the 16th (again that dreaded number) at
the age of fifty-nine. The number 16 was a warning of possible accident
or death, his mother-in-law Bessie had said (1960 added up to 16, as did
1942) shortly before Carole's plane crashed on January 16th, 1942, killing
Carole, Bessie and all aboard. On the night of the 16th of November, 1960,
Clark Gable, 'The King,' closed his eyes to sleep and never opened them
again. Among his bedside books at the hospital, was a copy of *GWTW*.

He was buried in a closed casket. Gable had told his fifth wife Kay "I
don't want a lot of strangers looking down at my wrinkles and my big fat
belly when I'm dead." He was laid to rest next to Carole, in a simple wall
crypt. David Selznick stood among the invited spectators, looking far
off into the distance in private thought — beyond the trees that towered
over the church. Fall leaves rustled and drifted to the ground as the wind
stirred among the eucalyptus.

Following Carole's death, Clark had lived in their home until his own
demise eighteen years later. In 1973 his widow, Kay, whom he had married
in 1955, sold the ranch. Today the two-story Connecticut farmhouse with
the gabled roof is surrounded by a development called The Clark Gable
Estates. The 'Estates' include two dedicated streets, Ashley Drive and Tara

Drive. Tourists, pursuing the ghost of Rhett Butler, cruise by the ranch and gaze wistfully at the home where Gable once tended his horses. And some even claim they have seen the ghost of Gable roaming through the house as if looking for someone. The exterior of their old home looks exactly the same as it did when Carole and Clark lived there, that they might be expected, at any moment, to walk out the front door of 4543 Tara Drive.

Movie people spend years of their lives creating dramatic and emotional situations for the fictional characters they play. Is it no wonder then that their personal lives are so often chaotic, as complicated as the characters they've invented. The lovers of *GWTW* are forever locked together — yet the people who played the roles were often torn apart.

To this day, friends and fans, colleagues and biographers, and most of the media have tried to fathom the twenty-year relationship of Vivien Leigh and Laurence Olivier. As the years have passed, many people who knew them have become less reticent to share their personal memories of the two. Many initially held back, fearing that what they might say would upset their own position with them, particularly after Olivier's knighthood (July 8, 1947) followed by his elevation to the peerage. Now, with both of them gone, numerous books have been written, with authors often taking different paths (i.e. points of view) though necessarily sometimes walking in each other's footsteps. One biographer, Jesse Lasky, Jr., visiting San Francisco with his wife and collaborator Pat (Silver), spoke with me in December of 1978 about their experiences and feelings relating to the Oliviers. Jesse Jr., the son of film pioneer Jesse L. Lasky, had written novels, volumes of poetry, plays — as well as screenplays for Cecil B. De Mille. A handsome and sensitive man, Jesse lived out his last years with Pat in London. He spoke of the Oliviers almost reverently. "I saw them for the first time together on the set of *Fire Over England* in 1936. I was deeply impressed by their beauty and the quality…of a kind of passion that seemed to surge through them. Then through the years one met them. We began to think about them as the most interesting couple in the world of theatre and film. The lovers whose romance and style was only seconded by the Duke and Duchess of Windsor. They had captivated everyone who entered their enchanted circle."

After three years of waiting, Vivien and Larry were finally married one minute after midnight on August 31st, 1940. Justice of the Peace Fred Harsh, in Santa Barbara, California, almost passed out declaring, "My God, it's Scarlett O'Hara!" As Anthony Burgess stated, "We are all movie struck." Attended by Katherine Hepburn and Garson Kanin, they were wed under a full moon, facing east towards England. "When Larry went back to England for the war," said George Cukor, "Vivien went with him unquestioningly, leaving her career in Hollywood when she could have been the biggest star in Hollywood and around the world."

"Larry is playing in the most important part of all, that of serving our country. I must be with him," she said.

From the day Vivien first read Tennessee William's play *A Streetcar Named Desire,* she set her sights on being the first British actress to play

Jesse Lasky, Jr. with wife Pat during my interview in San Francisco.

Blanch DuBois. Under Olivier's direction Vivien opened at London's
Aldwych Theatre on October 11, 1949. She was nothing less than a sensation. Audiences searched for something of Scarlett O'Hara to emerge
from somewhere in all her performances and in this they found her — and
now, from this point onward, they would seek out Blanche: a dual blend
of personalities. The part of the faded, shopworn southern belle, downcast

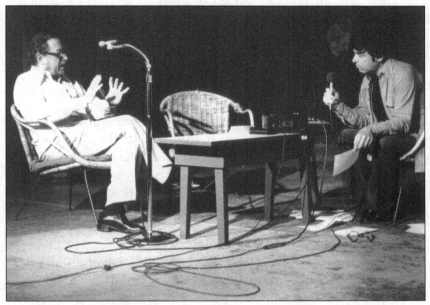

The author interviewing Tennessee Williams for NPR.

but resolved, Blanche could well have been a descendent of Scarlett; a
great grand-daughter who had lost the family plantation Bellerive (Tara).

Vying for the film role of Blanche were some high-powered actresses,
Bette Davis and Vivien's co-star from *GWTW,* Olivia de Havilland. Clearly
the part was meant for Vivien, with her own life's despair contributing
to her understanding of Blanche. Unlike Scarlett O'Hara, however, her
Blanche Du Bois is no longer young. She is a sexually disturbed woman
who lives in a world of illusion after her fragile universe begins to crumble.
Vivien's performance is unfailing, undeniably so to its final scene where
she is taken by kind strangers, the doctor and matron, to a mental asylum.

When Tennessee Williams was in San Francisco the winter of 1972,
I saw him almost daily over a period of several weeks. He was the play-
wright in residence, reworking his Two Character Play, and I was the
associate producer. He felt that of all of his plays transferred to the screen,

Streetcar was done the best…and as he told me, "The film had integrity, and to have Vivien retrieved for the generations is a great accomplishment." Tennessee, or Tom as those close to him called him, came to love Vivien Leigh and never forgot her kindness to his lover, Frank Merlo, during the last months of his life. Over his usual drink, Black Daniels, he elaborated, "She was the most profoundly lovely actress and woman I ever knew; a warm, generous person. She had no idea she was so ill the last time we met, but I could tell she hadn't long. I'm glad she went fast. Her film role as Blanche was all her own and quite genuine. But I liked her work in *The Roman Spring of Mrs. Stone* even better…"

As confided by three close friends:

Vivien suffered privately with her helplessness over Olivier's homosexual escapades (Danny Kaye in particular, as confirmed to me by David Thompson the Film Historian) Danny Kaye was assumed bisexual, like Olivier. Kaye was married for 47 years to songwriter and had a daughter, Dena. However, Donald Spoto, in his biography of Laurence Olivier, wrote that Kaye carried on an affair with the British actor in the 1950s.

The allegation was backed up by Michael Korda, editor in chief at Simon & Schuster, who said Olivier described the liaison in a draft of his memoirs, but was urged by his wife, actress Joan Plowright, to remove the references before publication.

The play that established the stereotype of the homosexual in the theatre was in Noel Coward's *The Green Bay Tree*, in 1933 starring Olivier. When he first met Vivien Leigh she became his obsession, and he carried to his grave an eternal torch for Vivien, the one true love of his life. Ironically, it was just as Vivien began to emerge from the depths of manic depression in the mid 1950s, after the Kaye affair had ended, that Olivier fell in love with Joan Plowright. The Olivier's divorced in 1960, and three months later the actor married Plowright.

If ever the old saying "opposites attract" is true, then this was the case with Lord Olivier, the son of a clergyman, and Danny Kaye, the son of a Brooklyn garment tailor. Although there was only six years difference between them, it was like Shakespeare goes Broadway. Brooding Hamlet meets zany clown. One thing they had in common was a tempestuous love-hate relationship with their wives. Namely, Leigh's nymphomania and declining health, were compounded by Olivier's bisexuality and guilt. And with Kaye, his wife Sylvia Fine, who managed his career, wrote his material and dominated his life. Privately, Olivier and Kaye could sympathize with one another.

...and her own flights into nymphomania. Blanche's loneliness, as it did Vivien in her manic moods, had plunged her into the depths of depravity. She knew that something in the haunted character of Blanche Du Bois had touched a wound deep within her soul, and she always defended Blanche. To her, Blanche was a delicately sensitive woman whose mind was shattered by the shock of finding that she had married a homosexual who committed suicide. Blanche was lost after that in a harsh, cruel world. Ravaged, envisioning magic, she stepped over into a world of fantasy. For her searing, heartbreaking portrayal, Vivien won her second Academy Award, March 20, 1952. For all the glory she paid a terrifying price. The cycle of her illness began in earnest; while filming *Elephant Walk* in Ceylon in February of 1953, she suffered a complete breakdown, accompanied by bouts of mania. While convalescing in Netherine Hospital in England that April, thieves broke into the Olivier home at Durham Cottage, stealing jewelry, furs and the Oscar won for 'Streetcar'. Two months later in June, burglars broke into Notley Abbey, the country home the Olivier's had bought in 1943, and stole the remainder of her jewelry. Lord Olivier issued an appeal through the press: "There is one piece she treasures most. A ruby ring I gave her when I came back from Hollywood to join the Navy. It's a sentimental thing. If she could only have it back. I think she'd be satisfied. Everyone knows Vivien has been ill, yet these men broke into her bedroom. They seem quite heartless. Among the missing objects was her wedding ring." Olivier's appeal was ignored — nothing was ever returned.

To everyone's surprise and astonishment, on July 12th, 1956, Vivien announced to the world that she was going to have a baby — but within weeks she suffered her second miscarriage.

"It is very easy to speculate and say that if the child had survived they would have gone on and on," Jesse Lasky replied in answer to my query. "They both desperately wanted a child. But the things that came between them — the shadows that fell were more complex than just the loss of that child. I know Olivier was terribly broken that they didn't have the child — as she was. The manic depression that followed, that was the key to a terrible growing darkness."

His wife Pat Silver added, "You asked why no one protected her from herself. The strange thing about Vivien was that no matter how ill she was, she never really showed it. People thought she was much better physically, than she was, until she would collapse even when she had a really serious breakdown on *Elephant Walk*. Olivier who was in Hollywood went to her, and with the help of friends took her back to England. She had been completely unconscious throughout most of the trip, yet, she got herself together and on her feet. She walked off the plane smiling carrying a huge bouquet of flowers and greeted the press. That kind of courage, that stamina — it was hard for the press to believe she was as ill as she was. She was taken to a convalescent home and Olivier was ordered away for a rest. Her illness was breaking his health down." After electric-shock therapy and some recuperation Vivien was always eager to get back to work, to be with friends and spend as much time as possible with her Larry. But the manic-depressive spells would reoccur with increasing frequency and intensity. In between these spells, she fought to keep his love alive. And she fought for what she believed in.

On July 10, 1957 Vivien led a protest march down the Strand in London to prevent the destruction of the 122-year-old St. James Theatre to make way for a block of offices. Two days later on July 12, she interrupted a session of the House of Lords to plead for its survival. Lord Blackforth, who was winding up his speech, was stopped in the middle of it when suddenly Lady Olivier stood up and cried out, "My Lords, I wish to protest against the St. James Theatre being demolished." No matter, on July 27, the proud old classical theatre was torn down. Even the fighting spirit of "Scarlett O'Hara" could not save it from the cold-hearted property investors.

Every time this writer visited England, I had always hoped that Vivien Leigh would be appearing in the West End, but I would invariably have to wait until she came to Broadway. On one particular trip to London, I waited by the statue of Charlie Chaplin, in Leicester Square, for actor Patrick Brock. Tall, white haired, and Irish with a thespian's flair, he arrived precisely on time, and we proceeded to lunch at an Indian restaurant next to the Empire Theatre, where he was obviously well known. After catching up I asked if he had ever met Vivien Leigh. His response was more that I had anticipated.

"In 1959 I was cast to play in support of Vivien Leigh in Olivier's production of Noel Coward's *Look After Lulu* at the Royal Court Theatre. We assembled onstage one summer morning for a reading with the director, Tony Richardson, and sat in a semi-circle, with Vivien Leigh in the center. Vivien was then brought along the line to meet her cast: Anthony Quayle and Robert Stephens who she knew, but the rest of us were unknown to her.

"Though we all had seen her brilliant screen work from the early Scarlett to the sad, mad Blanche Du Bois, we were admiring and not a little in awe of her. She was exquisitely dressed, a classic suit, discreet jewels, gloves. She always felt her hands were too big. A small woman, raven-haired with that beautiful dazzling face, Vivien was quiet and intent. When it was my turn, I murmured something about the privilege and pleasure of working with her. The lovely green eyes appraised me and that enchanting mouth broke into her cat-like smile. Suddenly there was a flurry of sound off-stage, and a young actress appeared late and apologetic. She was dressed not for a rehearsal but formally, for something like Ascot or a Royal garden-party with a huge picture hat, formal long gown and long, long gloves. The cynical actor next to me muttered, 'she won't last till lunchtime.' He was right! We had an unusually long break and after lunch, in her chair sat Muriel Forbes (the handsome wife of Sir Ralph Richardson) to play the second lead. During rehearsals Vivien was tireless and professional — mid-forties playing a girl of twenty — not a great stage actress. But a great screen actress, Claire Bloom, who had worked with Vivien, disagreed.

"Sir Noel Coward came to a London rehearsal and was funny, witty and kind. But around this time, something went wrong. Vivien became subdued and distraught. Rumors spread through the company — we all loved her. Olivier was asking for a divorce; she was resisting. We were silent and supportive. We played a week out of town, and then came the opening night. She had presents for all of us; mine was champagne and peaches. I bought her a green-leather engagement book for her dressing room. The first night was a glittering occasion. Katharine Hepburn came backstage to visit Vivien, Boris Karloff also appeared unexpectedly on our landing backstage, there talking shyly to my proud mother. Waiting on the crowded staircase was Olivier with Laurence Harvey.

"Laurence Harvey, born 1928 in Yomishkis, Lithuania, died 1973, was ambitious and scored a personal triumph in the title part of Henry V, in the 1958-59 Old Vic Tour of the US. He became a screen star with his perceptive performances as a ruthlessly ambitious young man in *Room at the Top*. He was a social climber to perfection and hung around Laurence Olivier. Harvey, twenty-one years Olivier's junior, was a known homosexual.

"Patrick Brock was the Equity deputy, so often he was called to Vivien's room to discuss company matters. I adored her and gradually we became friends. I escorted her to matinees of other plays. *[She felt at ease with Brock, who was gay and safe.]* One night she asked for me after the play, and when I arrived in her room she was sitting in front of her make-up table in a short pink satin dress, a-glitter with diamonds. 'I'm going to have supper with Larry,' she said and looked at me via the mirror. Then slowly…'it may be a difficult evening.' 'You look wonderful,' I said, 'and that's half the battle.' She looked at me, 'No, my dear, only a very small percentage of the battle.'

"The next night I arrived early at the theatre, as usual. As I got to the stage door, I saw her ahead of me. She was also always early. I recognized her mink coat; it was fall by now. I hastened to open the heavy door and got a tremendous shock. Gone was the sparkling beauty of the previous night. She was suddenly old-pale, her beautiful eyes pink with tears behind the dark glasses, her skin white and drawn. She greeted me quietly and I saw her to her dressing room. 'She can't play tonight,' I thought. 'She's ill.' The understudy was fine, but a sell-out house was expecting Vivien. I was wrong. She came down on-stage, as was her custom, to talk to us all (the cast) for five minutes before the curtain went up. But the usual gaiety and friendly questions were absent and never returned. Close-up on stage, one glimpsed the despair in that small, vividly-painted face and the panic in those lovely eyes. But bravely she went on with this romp of a farce."

Look After Lulu transferred from the Royal Court to the West End in September 1959. The Oliviers continued to pose affectionately together in Vivien's dressing room for reporters on the trail of the rumored break-up. Olivier eventually divorced her and married Joan Plowright. Vivien did a tour of Australia and one last film in Hollywood, *Ship of Fools*, a final play in New York, a musical with Jean Pierre Aumont, and then back to her English homes — to die. "And died of a broken heart," Brock said, "I've always been convinced."

It was the spring of 1960, four months after *Look After Lulu* closed, although Vivien herself had been highly praised by the critics for her performance and her "timeless beauty." Anxious to keep busy and trying to keep the demons away, she worked with an almost frantic tempo and went into a revival of Jean Giraudoux's play *Duel of Angels*, which came to New York, my hometown. She returned to Broadway, April 24, 1960.

I secured a ticket in advance as she always sold-out. When she first made her appearance as the diabolical Paola in *Duel of Angels*, the ovation was deafening. Her dark beauty was heightened by the vivid red gown she wore, and Mary Ure's blonde beauty playing the Virtue to her Vice was the perfect foil for her. She gave a brilliant portrayal while she was emotionally and physically at the lowest ebb of her life. Olivier called Vivien during rehearsals asking for a divorce to marry Joan Plowright, after twenty-five years. Onstage at the Helen Hayes Theatre she carried on with the sort of gallant courage as Scarlett O'Hara. In her dressing room, she wept uncontrollably.

Throughout the run Vivien had shock treatments every morning but went on to perform every night. Meanwhile she had heard from Olivier in London, persistently pleading for a divorce. After its New York engagement, the play went on tour to Los Angeles and, from there, to one of her favorite cities, San Francisco. When she returned to England she began looking for a new house, since Notley Abbey had been sold. Notley Abbey, a 22-room stone house set on 69 acres in Buckinghamshire had been their refuge. The Abbey had survived onslaughts for centuries and, when the Oliviers bought it in the 1940s, they were the golden couple, the idealized romantic couple. As were Scott and Zelda in the 1920s and Edward and Wallis in the 1930s, so were Larry and Vivien in the 1940s. They spent a fortune to restore and refurbish the house, and it was while at Notley Abbey that Olivier was knighted by the Queen. It was also there that they shared both glorious and tragic times. During 1954-55 Vivien remained at Notley under medical care, fighting to overcome her fear of becoming permanently insane. (Today people suffering from manic depression are held on steadier ground, thanks to lithium).

When the time finally came to discuss their impending divorce and selling Notley, Vivien returned there alone from London and waited for a call from Lord Olivier, her Larry, that never came. So their twelfth-century country home was sold. The Abbey still stands as a shrine to their love, occupied by others, but always recalled in association with its romantic past. In the fall of that year, Vivien parted from Olivier and began looking for a new home. She found it in Tickerage Mill, an elegant five-bedroom Queen Anne mill-house at Uckfield in Sussex. Hidden in the valley of the river, Uck Tickeridge Mill is set in ninety acres of woodland and streams. She was happy that it was surrounded by water. Along with her treasured antiques and prized paintings, Vivien found a special niche for her two Oscars, one for Scarlett and one for Blanche (a replaced duplicate) — those haunting ladies who followed her like shadows. Then what Vivien prayed would never come to pass — did on December 2, 1960. After twenty years of marriage, the Oliviers were divorced. In a last attempt to win him back, she flew to New York just weeks later on March 8, 1961, where he was appearing on stage in *The Entertainer* with her rival, Joan Plowright. She held out for a miracle, but it was a hopeless gesture. She left New York heartbroken but resolved to keep her promise to attend the re-release premier of *Gone With the Wind* in Atlanta for the Civil War Centennial in 1961. Olivia de Havilland was the only other major player who would be there. 'Scarlett' would not be reunited with her Rhett, as Clark Gable had died just eight months before. Clark, the gentlemanly-ruffian who had taught her to play backgammon during intervals on *GWTW* and never won a game from her. Aboard the same aircraft sat a forlorn looking man, appearing much older than his sixty-one years. David O. Selznick had been transformed by his cinema monument.

An incurable romantic, Selznick never bettered his making of *GWTW* at age thirty-seven and, in his private life, had observed a dictum of his father, "Live expensively. Live beyond your means if you have confidence in yourself. Money isn't that important." But money *was* important and Selznick-International had by this time gone to Hollywood's Valhalla. Now at the twilight of a long and fabled career, Selznick glanced reflectively at his gold wrist watch, a melancholy reminder of the end of filming on *GWTW* that bore the inscription in John Hay (Jock) Whitney's handwriting "David — Christmas 1939. Praise de Lawd." John Whitney, with his cousin Cornelius Vanderbilt Whitney, helped finance the development of Technicolor and Cinerama, and they co-produced a half-dozen David O. Selznick pictures, including *GWTW* and *Rebecca*. Selznick-International, formed in 1935 with the backing of Whitney and his friends, was dissolved in August 1940 with profound regret "that the risks involved to world conditions made it desirable for us to take this step." A new firm David O. Selznick Productions, Inc. would assume its obligations. In 1947, Selznick divorced Irene Mayer and within two years married his obsession, actress Jennifer Jones. Always the exemplar, he didn't like to hear his other films preferred to his fabulous *GWTW*. "There is nothing that infuriates me so much. It was such a stupendous undertaking, anything else, no matter we'll ever make, will always seem insignificant after that." But he tried. And so the old order was gone, but there was nothing to replace it: thus the past is transformed and glorified.

Still, by 1949 his company had gone into liquidation, his star contracts, distribution rights, even the costumes, were sold. Disenchanted, he made the oft-quoted comment to Ben Hecht, worth repeating: "Hollywood's like Egypt, full of crumbled pyramids. It'll never come back...there might have been good movies if there had been no movie industry. Hollywood might have become the center of a new human experience if it hadn't been grabbed by a little group of bookkeepers." On June 22, 1965, at age sixty-three, David O. Selznick was felled by a coronary at his lawyer's office and died shortly afterwards. With him went a certain style of opulence, devotion to classical literature, and regard for audience intelligence. The Selznick style achieved its apotheosis in *GWTW*.

Selznick kept looking for another *GWTW* for his obsession, Jennifer Jones; he had changed her name and destiny. Now he wanted to immortalize her in a monumental motion picture. He felt that Leo Tolstoy's *War and Peace* would be it. It never happened. The phantom *GWTW* hovered over them to the end of their days. Jennifer Jones, a chronic depressive, drove to a four-hundred foot cliff near Malibu two years after Selznick's death to end her life. She was found unconscious near shallow surf and survived.

For all its subsequent good fortune, *GWTW* branded many of its participants for life. Fame, beauty, and talent were not enough to keep the demons at bay. A star was born in Vivien Leigh and Selznick became Hollywood's new wonder boy. For others, the historic production swept over them like a tempest, leaving them buried in its wake where only the ghosts wander. First, Sidney Howard, on his farm in Massachusetts;

then F. Scott Fitzgerald, who died of a heart attack in Hollywood at age forty-four. Three years later Leslie Howard — who had always wanted to put Ashley Wilkes to rest — was gone, too. On a mission for the British Council on June 1, 1943, Howard was to lecture on Hamlet in Spain and Portugal as part of his schedule of war activities. He was aboard a commercial London-Lisbon airliner BOAC flight that Nazi aircraft shot down over the Bay of Biscay, believing Hitler's arch enemy, Prime Minister Winston Churchill, was a passenger. No trace of the plane with thirteen passengers aboard, including Leslie Howard, and a crew of four was ever found. The next year, on March 22, 1944, the Little Napoleon of agents, Myron Selznick, died of a heart attack, at age forty-five, for all his power an empty man and only remembered for thrusting a British girl into the part of the notorious Southern belle Scarlett O'Hara. Then in 1949, Victor Fleming died. His films after *GWTW* were notable failures. Vivien could think back on the fights, on-the-set quarrels between them, usually with Vivien in tears and Fleming in rage. Aunt Pittypat, Laura Hope Crews, died in 1942, at sixty-two. The thieving Yankee soldier Scarlett shot on the stairs at Tara, Paul Hurst, passed away in 1953. Rand Brooks, who wanted to be remembered for his more assertive roles, was forever tied to his Charles Hamilton *GWTW* character, even in the headline of his obituary.sixty-four years later.

Upon landing, Vivien was startled out of her reverie by a crowd of fans, many of them from the 1939 premiere. The mob at Atlanta airport loudly welcomed her "home." "Scarlett, we love you," they shouted along Peachtree Street that night when her limousine drove by on its way to the Lowe's Grand. Vivien cried all the way through the picture, seeing all who had gone before her, and particularly when Gerald O'Hara, silhouetted alongside the twenty-eight-year-old Scarlett against the evening sky at Tara, sets forth to her the meaning of the one thing she has left when everything else is wrecked. She had Tara and, within reach possibly, even Rhett. What had Vivien, at forty-seven, without Nutley — without Larry? The film, haunted of memories, filled her with sadness. Its fantasy had become her reality.

Margaret Mitchell had written to a friend, "I'm going to die in a car crash. I feel certain of this." On Thursday August 11, 1949, Margaret and her husband drove a few blocks to catch an evening's performance of the British film *A Canterbury Tale* at the Atlanta Peachtree Art Theatre. Tara's theme was playing on the car radio, of all things. Since they were in a hurry to make the start of the show, Margaret parked on the street across from the theatre to save time. When the couple was just beyond the road's dividing line, a car driven by an off-duty taxi driver suddenly sped toward them. Margaret panicked and leaving her husband in the middle of the street ran back towards the curb. The drunken driver swerved and skidded sixty feet before hitting the tiny woman. This happened not far from the Grand at 660 Peachtree Street, which frequently showed *GWTW* for benefit performances, and just a few blocks from the Windsor House at 979 Crescent Drive, where she had once lived and written 90% of her novel. She never regained consciousness, and died five days later on August 16th (16 again!) of brain injuries. She was forty-eight. Mitchell was buried in Oakland Cemetery under a magnolia tree, her grave marked with a plain white stone engraved simply "Margaret Mitchell Marsh."

Elvis Presley was a year old when *GWTW* was published. As a young man he examined the movie many times over, even affecting a Rhett Butler look with dyed black hair and sideburns. His Memphis home, Graceland, a fantasy-like Tara, was his ultimate goal. The cult hero died at forty-two on Tuesday, August 16th, 1977. It was the exact day and date as Margaret Mitchell's death.

On the morning of October 26, 1952, Hattie McDaniel passed away at age fifty-seven at the Motion Picture Home and Hospital in Woodland Hills, California. Almost fifty years later, she got her final wish. She requested in her will to be buried at the Hollywood Memorial Park Cemetery. "I desire a white casket and a white shroud; white gardenias in my hair, together with a white gardenia blanket and a pillow of red roses." But when she died in 1962 of breast cancer, the Los Angeles cemetery did not take blacks. She was buried instead at Angelus-Rosedale Cemetery. When the new owners of the Hollywood cemetery renamed it Hollywood Forever, they installed a memorial to recognize McDaniel. She was Mammy to the world and proud of it, signing her autograph Hattie "Mammy" McDaniel. In the Los Angeles Movieland Wax Museum — and also in Madame Tussauds in London — she is there as Mammy, along with Clark Gable as Rhett and Vivien Leigh as Scarlett.

In 1955, Ona Munson, who played Belle Watling, took an overdose of sleeping pills at age forty-eight, leaving behind a suicide note. George Reeves, first seen at the O'Hara plantation as one of the Tarleton twins, later to become a TV star with the *Superman* series, died in 1959 at age forty-five — his death still a mystery. Was it suicide or murder? His death on June 16th (16 again), 1959, however, was ruled a suicide. Scarlett threw the red dirt of Tara into the face "of the white trash" Emmy Slattery. The actress in the role, Isabel Jewell, became another victim of Hollywood. After *GWTW,* her career declined in the 1940s, she was out of work in the

1950s, and she was arrested in 1959 in Las Vegas on bad-check charges. During the 1961 Atlanta Revival of *GWTW,* she was arrested and sent to jail on a drunk driving charge. She died in 1972 at age sixty-three.

At the Ball following the screening, Vivien once again danced with the Governor of Georgia and the mayor of Atlanta. She talked anima-

Eric: *'My ma would wear me out with a cornstalk if she found out I came to your place, Belle.'* Belle: *'Well, at any rate, you got your hat off!'*

tedly with Margaret's brother Stephens Mitchell and smiled charmingly at everyone who approached her. It was a reprise of 1939, for those who were there the memories were rich and resonant. Vivien left Atlanta, on this her last visit, with bittersweet feelings. She returned to England on March 17th, 1962 and on that same day Olivier married Joan Plowright in a civil ceremony in Connecticut. A few weeks later, in April, Vivien was robbed of her handbag containing her passport, rings Olivier had given her, and her gold cigarette lighter in the shape of a star, the one Selznick had given her as a memento of Scarlett. Driven by loneliness for Olivier and a need for the love of an audience, which kept her going, on the 12th of July she led the Old Vic Company on a tour of Australia, New Zealand and Latin America. She was enormously popular wherever she went. After all, who didn't know "Scarlett?" Several months later, still driving herself, she opened on Broadway in a musical of *Tovarich,* on

March 18, 1963, at the Broadway Theatre, in New York. The critics hailed her as "one of the crown jewels" and she won the Tony Award, Broadway's equivalent to the Oscar for her performance.

After ten months in the show, doctors advised her to go back to London. As she explained, "I suppose it is silly at my age to go jumping up and down doing the Charleston with my heart pounding, bathed in

The Tarlington twins on the steps of Tara, signed by Frederick 'Fred' Crane.

sweat, for six hours (matinees included) at a time. But I did it and I loved it. I knew I would be ill, but I was not given a holiday because the show had to go on. And then — it happened."

I was lucky to have seen her in *Tovarich* before her breakdown forced her to leave the show on September 30th 1963. She returned to London for treatment and then on to Tickerage Mill to recuperate.

Compulsive to keep busy and constantly sought after, she returned to New York in Anton Chekov's *Ivanov* in May of 1966.

I went to see her as the beautiful, doomed, consumptive Anna. For some reason, perhaps feeling this may be the last time I would see her, I felt I had to contact her. I sent a telegram to her dressing room at the Schubert Theatre. Though she was still going through the routine of electroshock treatments every morning, appearing on stage that night, she responded with a note addressed to my office at Lincoln Center where I was working for the New York City Opera and Ballet Companies, at times with impresario Jean Dalrymple.

Encouraged by her warm response, I managed to secure her private telephone number and impulsively called one day. I hesitated too long…

the woman who answered identified herself as Joan Fontaine, who informed me that Vivien had left for England. Shortly afterwards Vivien was again stricken with a reoccurrence of the tuberculosis, first diagnosed in 1945, and was forced to postpone rehearsals for her next play, *A Delicate Balance*. A sense of urgency came over me that I cannot explain. I was determined to meet with her face-to-face, if only for a moment. I planned a trip to London from New York, intending to arrive backstage with a letter of introduction around my birth date, July 12th, but to my enduring sorrow, on Friday the 7th of July, 1967, she was found dead — alone in her bedroom at 54 Eaton Square. She was discovered by her loving and loyal companion throughout her remaining years, Jack Merivale, face down on the floor near her bed: a four poster canopied reproduction of the one at Tara in *GWTW*. On the nightstand were Olivier's old letters, clearly read and re-read, and the ever-present silver framed photograph of a young Olivier — her Larry.

John Merivale was an actor who often played English Gentlemen with a stiff upper lip. Born into a theatrical family in Toronto, Merivale entered movies in 1933. However it was in 1938 that he appeared on stage in London and met Vivien Leigh. After her separation from Olivier, they began an affair. They acted together in 1958 in the play *Duel of Angels*, repeating his role in the revival in New York. Again with Vivien

160 EAST 72nd STREET
NEW YORK 21, NEW YORK

June 14, 1966

Dear Mr. Arcieri:

I was most touched and encouraged by your really charming
telegram.

Thank you for your very kind
thought.

With all good wishes,

Yours sincerely,

[signature]

VIVIEN LEIGH

Mr. Eugene Arcieri
New York City Center and State Theatre
New York, New York

Reply from Vivien Leigh.

he appeared in *Ivanov* on Broadway. When Vivien and Olivier divorced in 1961, they lived together until her death in 1967. He had come back into her life when she longed for love, understanding, and companionship. Merivale gave her all these, knowing there would always be the live ghost of Laurence Olivier between them. Twenty-three years later, he died at age seventy-two.

Leigh and Merivale.

The news of Vivien Leigh's death shocked her fans around the world. I, too, felt the loss and postponed my trip. A Londoner scratched the words, "A great actress forever and ever. We vote you the young at heart and a true beauty" on a column outside the house where she lived. Another personality, Bea Arthur, of The TV show *The Golden Girls,* told the National Enquirer that when she rented the Flat at 54 Eaton Square where Vivien died, she had to move out because the ghost of Vivien Leigh, dressed as Scarlett O'Hara, haunted the place. Bea collapsed and had to see a doctor after being driven out by ghost in the London apartment she leased from Mick Jagger and Jerry Hall. "The first night I stayed in this flat I found the ghost of Vivien Leigh, dressed as Scarlett O'Hara, roaming through the living room."

A requiem Mass was held in the Roman Catholic Church of St. Mary's on July 12th at 10 o'clock for immediate family, the coffin covered with her favorite white roses from the garden at Tickerage Mill. Vivien's will specified that she be cremated, and that meant at the time that a Catholic burial was out of the question. She was cremated at the Golders Green Crematorium. Vivien's mother accompanied Jack Merivale down to the country to carry out her last wish — that her ashes be scattered over the lake at Tickerage. (Or were they?) As the years passed, every photo of Vivien told a story. Perhaps, with the exception of one. There is a photograph taken of her at twilight at Tickerage shortly before she died. She is seen sitting by the lake staring off into some place known only to her.

Five weeks after her death, on August 15, 1967, at 11 a.m., actors from all over London gathered at the Parish Church of St. Martin-in-the-Fields for their own memorial service. Mounting the twenty-seven steps were some of the best-known names in the British Theatre: Dame Peggy Ashcroft, Anna Neagle, Emlyn Williams, Terrance Rattigan, Sir John Gielgud, Leigh Holman — Vivien's first husband, her last lover, Jack Merivale, and her mother, Gertrude. Hundreds of friends filled the intimate church. About an hour before the service began, Sir Laurence Olivier slipped in alone at the back. Sheltered by a pillar, he stood gravely with head bent. The prayers of St. Francis of Assisi, which were by Vivien's bedside when she died, were spoken by Lady Redgrave.

I eventually arrived in London in late August and soon found myself at Trafalgar Square, across from St. Martin-in-the-Fields. I visited the Vicar's office, hoping to find out what I could about the memorial service and to inquire where I might pay my respects. The following may seem unbelievable, even dreamlike. It has haunted me to this day, but I swear to its truth. I was seated in the Vicar's waiting room, outside his office, when a woman approached me, seemingly from out of nowhere. For some reason, I suppose because it was on my mind, when I spoke to her I said how surprised I was to learn that Miss Leigh had been cremated.

"Oh, no," she said almost in a whisper, "No — she is buried in the lake at Tickerage. Her coffin lies beneath the surface — held down by chains.

Church and commemorative plaque.

She feared fire but loved the water. She was a water sign astrologically. She was happiest within distance of water..." That was it! I cannot describe the woman; that's all I can remember of that fleeting experience so many years ago. On leaving the office, I walked down the side steps into the church and sat for awhile in one of the rear pews before I walked outside into Trafalgar Square's busy crowds and London's traffic.

A decade later, when I told Jesse Lasky, Jr., and his wife Pat about it at the Clift Hotel in San Francisco, they looked at me dumbstruck. We left it there, although I can still listen to their comments on tape. I never mentioned it again to anyone after that. It all seemed too unreal, but the woman in the Vicar's office waiting room and what she revealed to me remains very real to me-to this day. What Vivien Leigh returned to most often was her love of the sea, to be near water, and whether she willed it or not, she saw much more in it and drew much more out of its surface appearances than so many others have done. She was somehow able to make its depth felt and, through its waters, to explore human themes as far apart as those of her childhood until her death. Water was healing, restful, spiritual, against tragic adversaries. The last, at Tickerage, could also have been seen as oblivion, the chill green shroud.

"Meditation and water," wrote Herman Melville, "are wedded forever." It was the lake at Tickerage that transformed an ordinary landscape for Vivien into a rejuvenating refuge, a shimmering oasis of peaceful contemplation. Who knew what limits lie within her imagination? She sat by the lake, often staring into silent depths. A single raindrop or the softest breeze sending ripples cascading to its outer edge. She studied the light on the water; the darker the color, the deeper it seemed, her mood darkening, deepening accordingly.

Early on Tuesday, July 11, 1989, a priest was called to minister to Lord Olivier, who had died, surrounded by those who loved him, at the age of eighty-two, carrying to his grave a torch for the one true love of his life — Vivien Leigh. Ironically, it was just as she was beginning to emerge from the depths of her manic depression, in the mid 1950s (TB claimed her life at fifty-three) that he fell for the actress Joan Plowright, whom he married three months after his divorce in 1960. "Until the day he died, Larry was obsessed with Vivien," said an insider. Another confided, "He couldn't help himself. Even twenty-two years after her death, she still had the power to twist him in knots. He loved her intensely (but) despite the mental torture she put him through he could never shake the nagging guilt he felt over her mental illness." It was impossible for him not to believe that he was somehow the cause of her disturbances. He wrote in his autobiography, "that they were due to some fault in me." His bi-sexuality perhaps. He was tortured by memories of Vivien in his old age, confiding to friends that his marriage to Plowright was a mistake and often referring to her as Vivien. The past catches up with us all — you can't escape it! But what of the love story — a love story oblivious to the calendar and the ambivalence and yearnings that motivated it? Could it have been otherwise? Joseph Conrad wrote: "If two beings thrown together, mutually attracted resist the necessity, fail in understanding and voluntarily stop short of the embrace, in the noblest meaning of the word, they are committing a sin against life, the call of which is simple...perhaps sacred." Their romance was an entity in and of itself, neither detracted from the future nor destroyed by the past.

Right after the death of her dear friend Olivier, a pal since the 1939 premiere of *GWTW*, Olivia de Havilland lost another close friend of fifty-four years, Bette Davis, just weeks later. The double deaths left such emotional scars on Olivia that she could not attend the 50th anniversary celebration of *GWTW* that year, 1989. Sadly she remembered how terrible she felt at the 1967 gathering of the *GWTW* cast. None of her co-stars, including Vivien, Leslie, Howard and Clark Gable, had lived to be there with her. Olivia's twilight years have been steeped in tragedy. Her children's health problems have taken their toll. But the ninety-three-year-old actress continues to fight her battles alone with courage and with "faith in God." She was the survivor! Olivia seemed to escape the clutches of being frozen as a sentimental keepsake of *GWTW*, as happened to so many others connected with the picture; instead she enhanced and developed her skills to go to greater achievements. Unlike, say, Evelyn Keyes, who played the pouty Suellen O'Hara, whose sister Scarlett steals her long-time boyfriend and married him just to pay the taxes on the plantation. When I met Keyes on October 12, 1978, to interview her for NPR, she was promoting her first memoir, *Scarlett O'Hara's Younger Sister*. Always claiming that *GWTW* was all she would be remembered for, she died on July 4, 2008, at her home in Montecito, California at ninety-one.

It was around this time I also interviewed Miss de Havilland. She was lovely, appealing with her sly, feminine sense of humor and exacting intelligence. She was in San Francisco to promote the restored version of *The Adventures of Robin Hood*. Our interview took place in her hotel suite, with reporters from local papers backed up behind me and a television crew setting up. As I began to record, the moment she spoke, the room became silent. Following preliminaries, I maneuvered the conversation into her *GWTW* years. DeHavilland told me, "I was twenty-two years of age when I began filming *GWTW* and turned twenty-three on the very last day of shooting, July1,1939." She acknowledged "the industry that created people like me when we made *GWTW* is gone." I spoke to her of my visit to Atlanta many years before when I lived in New York. While visiting the Margaret Mitchell gravesite, I learned that, in accordance with her instructions, most of her correspondence and papers, including

Alfred Hitchcock, Eric Stacey, Reggie Callow — Table talk for Rebecca.

the manuscript of *GWTW,* had been destroyed, except for some pages preserved to authenticate her authorship.

There was surprisingly little to commemorate Atlanta's most famous citizen. "I'm sorry," she replied, "because I think some shrines are very wholesome and good for people. It would have been nice to visit Margaret Mitchell's house and see her personal effects, out of regard and respect for her, and what she created for us all to enjoy, which was that remark-able book, and from it, the film. In Feb 9, 1981, she had said, "Surviving time and change, *GWTW* now stands as a monument to the magic of the movies." I tried to stimulate some as-yet-unrevealed insight into her making of *GWTW* and the actors she had worked with. From her wist-ful expression, the distance behind those brown eyes, I could tell that I was probing too deeply into her private thoughts — areas she preferred, at that moment, to keep to herself. She went on just to say, to my query "One can only imagine what personal memories cross your mind when you see *GWTW* over again after so much that has happened in-between," simply an almost whispered "Yes."

Memories that could not help but include the crazy times with assistant

Reggie Callow, Eric Stacey, Joan Fontaine, sneaking a snack during a break, filming Rebecca.

director Eric Stacey on *GWTW.* Unfortunately, I met Miss de Havilland before I had become involved with the history of Eric Stacy's *GWTW* work and before I met his widow, Fran Stacey, who allowed me to take a close look into her husband's memorabilia, which captured his fellow workers in candid moments, languishing in the garage of their home. I was mesmerized, gazing into this lost world. I felt like an archeologist. The documentation, the photos — it was like coming across buried treasure.

Near the end of shooting on *GWTW,* Eric had to switch over from scenes with Olivia to those with her sister Joan Fontaine and Vivien's lover Olivier for *Rebecca.* Selznick needed Stacey's expertise with the new British director Alfred Hitchcock. *Variety* (November 2, 1939) reported that Eric moved into "top pilot" spot to handle filming of Fontaine and Olivier in a sequence authored by himself. Hitchcock felt some connecting footage was needed, so Eric wrote action and dialogue which was read to Selznick, in New York, over the phone for his approval.

On September 27th, Eric was taken off *Rebecca* as Selznick had to have him back on *GWTW* for additional scenes with Gable and Leigh.

After the dissolution of Selznick International, 1940, Eric worked for Cecil. B. De Mille on *North West Mounted Police* before signing a contract with Warner Bros. On December 5, 1942 Selznick wrote:

DAVID O. SELZNICK
CULVER CITY, CALIFORNIA

December 5, 1942

To Whom It May Concern:

Eric Stacey was associated with me for a number of years as assistant director and unit manager. These were posts of considerable responsibility, and doubly so with my organization because of its being an independent operation in which many duties of an important nature fell to Stacey that in larger plants would be handled by the executive office. Not the least among his activities were those connected with "Gone With the Wind," a picture making extraordinary demands on the position held by Stacey.

Stacey's duties were of an executive nature, involving the management of very large numbers of people, location trips, etc.; and he performed these with such skill as to cause me to carry him on the payroll for a number of years, even during periods between pictures when there was little for him to do.

It is obvious that I would not have given him this responsibility had I other than the highest regard for his character and integrity.

I should think that he would make excellent officer material for any motion picture branch of the Armed Forces, combat or otherwise.

Very truly, yours,

David O. Selznick

dos:fli

At Warner Bros. head of production/studio manager Eric worked with Gary Cooper, (Sgt, York), James Cagney, Cary Grant, Humphrey Bogart, Bette Davis, and again with Olivia de Havilland. He supervised Doris Day's first movie, *Romance on the High Seas,* and several pictures with Ronald Reagan.

Because of his work with Warner contract player Irene Manning, I was eventually to meet his wife, Fran, many years after Eric's death; and

Joan Fontaine, Laurence Olivier, Eric Stacey — Picnic scene set-up from Rebecca.

that was how I gained access to his career files.

Fifteen years after joining Warner Bros., Eric resigned in 1956 as head of production, because of "incomplete contractual arrangements." He free-lanced with other studios for a while and then went on to become unit production manager at 20th Century-Fox. Having just completed his latest picture, *The Only Game in Town,* with Elizabeth Taylor and Warren Beatty, on May 1, 1969, Eric was en route to a shooting location in Rosamond, California for *Run Shadow Run* (released in 1970 as *Cover Me Babe*). Studio driver Newall Haskins was driving Eric to the feature film's first day of production. Haskins said he did not see or hear the approaching Southbound train at a Southern Pacific crossing and was almost across when the speeding train hit their station wagon at 10:45 a.m. They were both taken to Antelope Valley Hospital in Rosamond, where Haskins was treated with relatively minor injuries. Eric succumbed at 12:05 p.m., dead at the age of sixty-five. In her home in North Hollywood, Fran Stacey heard the news on the radio. She ran from the house into the back garden, and screamed and kept screaming until she mercifully collapsed.

Caricature of Eric as director.

EPILOGUE

Have you ever looked back and wondered whatever became of those few special people in your life from days gone by? Remembered the times you've longed to see that face, hear that voice that you've loved and missed? Imagined a reunion with the past — escapism, perhaps? But Americans feed the growth of movie memorabilia stores and mail-order houses in droves, submerging today's worries in yesteryear's more innocent charms. The age of nostalgia, analysts say, is partly a creation of weariness of — and with — the "now generation," and partly the lingering effect of the nationally-divisive wars and constantly-emerging political corruptions and scandals; all contributing to a general malaise and moral instability of our times. Today's interest takes in the last eighty years, though focusing most sharply on a span that runs from the 1930s to the 1960s — the Elvis and Marilyn years. America's continuing love affair with yesterday shows up at the cash register, which keeps it alive and in demand. Memorabilia sold at auction now has a world-wide market. Hollywood's Classic Oldies are like gold. In the past years, it has been men who bought the collectibles. Dick Purtan bought Gable's copy of the 1939 *GWTW* script at Christie's auction house for $220,000. The grey wool coat Gable wore as Rhett Butler was acquired by Keith Hutson, who owns a chain of Taco Bells but won't reveal what he paid for the coat. Vivien Leigh's Oscar for *GWTW* fetched $510,000 at Sotheby's auction. The Academy of Motion Picture Arts and Sciences, which hands out the Oscars every year, tried to block the sale, saying the Oscar statuettes were never intended to be articles of trade; but a judge disagreed, clearing the way for the Oscars to be sold. The Academy claimed that two years before his death in 1960, Gable signed a standard contract giving it first right to buy the statuette for $10 if it was ever sold. Christie's claims the signature on the agreement was a fake. Fans eager for a piece of *GWTW* got their chance in 1996 in Concord, Georgia. A K. C. Bassham sold one-inch-by-three-inch pieces of the Tara plantation facade used in the 1939 movie. A piece of history is gone when portions of Scarlett's Tara go on sale for $199 each, when newly-available remnants of those few months of shooting at Selznick International in 1939 went filtering in for scrutiny, evaluation and cataloging on their way into the hands of eager collectors, to the "going, going, gone" of the auctioneer's gavel.

[Author's note: To the best of my knowledge, the sale of the Tara façade never took place. Bassham advertised the pieces of the façade, but Betty Talmadge, who actually owned the façade, denied that a deal was ever reached.]

A buyer and college professor from Alabama heard about the George Cukor auction at Butterfields, San Francisco, in 1982, and could barely wait to place his bid. Then he spotted a photograph of Vivien Leigh in the catalogue with its inscription "Love to my darling George." "I knew God meant me to have this," he said. "I still haven't come down to earth." Fred Crane, who portrayed the other Tarleton brother, Brent, in the film, sold his hard-bound 1938 edition of Margaret Mitchell's novel, signed by twenty-three members of the cast and crew. According to the auctioneer at Camden House L.A., Crane's mother bought the book and made him take it to the set for signatures. It sold for $30,000.

"What do we care if we were expelled from college, Scarlett? The war's going to start any day now, so we'd have left college anyhow!" As Brent Tarleton, one of Scarlett O'Hara's suitors, Fred Crane spoke the opening lines in *Gone with the Wind* in a scene on the front porch of Tara, with Vivien as Scarlett and George Reeves as his twin, Stuart. And so began and ended Fred Crane's film career. Crane was said to be the oldest surviving adult male cast member of *GWTW*. He died at the age of ninety in August 2008. Crane told the *Atlanta Journal Constitution* in 2007, "I'm just a small shard in a grand mosaic." When he was cast in the picture, the twenty year old commented, "It was a matter of being in the right place at the right time." A New Orleans native, his mother decided that he should try Hollywood. She gave him $50 and a one-way train ticket. He had connections: his cousin, former silent film actress, Leatrice Joy. In making the film, "twin brothers" Crane and Reeves became good friends. Reeves died in 1959. It was ruled a suicide, but Crane said, "someone shot him to death." His career ventured off into television and radio, and in 2000 Crane and his fifth wife bought an antebellum mansion in Barnesville, a town south of Atlanta. After making renovations, they turned it into a bed and breakfast, complete with a *Gone With the Wind* museum with artifacts from the film. However in 2007, due to Crane's medical problems, the couple auctioned off his home and its memorabilia. Yet, *GWTW* followed him to the grave. His obituaries all began describing his opening scene in *GWTW*...a few minutes of immortality.

"Brooklyn's Scarlett," Susan Hayward, who lost out on the role but screen tested for it many times, signed a studio portrait in purple ink on September 6, 1939. It sold at Ray Anthony's Autograph Co. in Beverly Hills for $1,000.00. And, lest we forget, Bill Clinton's favorite movie is *GWTW*.

The grand era of filmmaking is gone, as are the studio bosses and others who made their decisions and worked from gutsy instinct and a boot-strap; but those who contributed to *GWTW*'s creation live on in cherished memory — those frontiersmen and women of the industry who were involved in the making of the motion-picture, particularly the skilled cameramen, sound technicians, and the hundreds of people behind the scenes. Even with its strong romantic overtones, *GWTW* nevertheless qualifies in its own way as a Civil War documentary, based on recollections of the greatest collective tragedy yet to befall the American people in their own land. As the author wrote, "Chivalry took its last bow." Idolized as it is, *Gone With the Wind* will be able to withstand retrospection for another half century.

In the Sunday Pink section of *The San Francisco Chronicle*, August 8, 2008, is the movie critic Mick LaSalle's column, where he answers questions sent in by its readers:

Mary Ann Lahann, from Newcastle wrote: Hello Mick: What movie sold the most tickets (yes, ever!) Not highest grosses, since every time ticket prices go up, there are a new winner in that category.

Hello Mary: Even before I checked, I knew the answer to this one: "*Gone With the Wind.*"

What is your life? For you are a mist that appears for a little time and then vanishes. We are but of yesterday and know nothing, for our days on earth are a shadow. Therefore, man does not live by time alone. We can stand outside our present time and imagine ourselves ahead in the future or back in the past. Within your memories enjoy the past. You don't want to live there, but it's nice to visit now and then to look back as you move ahead to the future. And another day.

INDEX

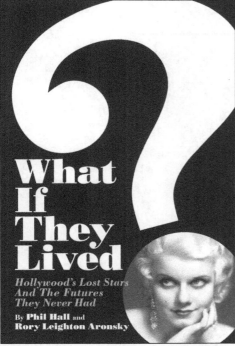

CPSIA information can be obtained
at www.ICGtesting.com
Printed in the USA
BVHW091955231221
624634BV00003B/59